1599   Moved to Southwark near t[...]
       which he and his company had recently erected.

1602   Extensive purchases of property and land in Strat-
       ford.

1602–4   Lodged with Mountjoy, a Huguenot refugee and
       a maker of headdresses, in Cripplegate, London.
       Helped to arrange a marriage between Mary
       Mountjoy and Stephen Belott, her father's appren-
       tice.

1603   His company became the King's Majesty's Players
       under royal patronage.

1607   His daughter Susanna married Dr John Hall.

1608   Birth of Shakespeare's grand-daughter Elizabeth
       Hall.

1610   Shakespeare possibly returned to live in Stratford.

1613   Purchase of the Gatehouse in Blackfriars. Burning
       of the Globe Theatre during the première of *Henry
       VIII*.

1616   Marriage of his daughter Judith to Thomas Quiney
       in Lent for which they were excommunicated.

25 March, 1616   Shakespeare altered the draft of his will
       presumably to give Judith more security in view
       of her husband's unreliability and his pre-marital
       misconduct with another woman. His will also
       revealed his strong attachment to his Stratford
       friends, and above all his desire to arrange for the
       establishment of his descendants.

23 April, 1616   Death of Shakespeare.

1623   Publication of the First Folio edition of Shake-
       speare's plays collected by his fellow actors Heminge
       and Condell to preserve 'the memory of so worthy
       a friend'.

THE MERCHANT
OF VENICE

In series with this book

TWELFTH NIGHT

THE MERCHANT OF VENICE

A MIDSUMMER NIGHT'S DREAM

KING HENRY IV PART ONE

ANTONY AND CLEOPATRA

ROMEO AND JULIET

AS YOU LIKE IT

JULIUS CÆSAR

KING HENRY V

THE TEMPEST

MACBETH

HAMLET

OTHELLO

Also edited by Dr. J. H. Walter

HENRY V (Arden Shakespeare)

CHARLEMAGNE (Malone Society)

LAUNCHING OF THE MARY (Malone Society)

THE MERCHANT
OF VENICE

Edited by

J. H. WALTER

M.A., PH.D.

Formerly Headmaster
Minchenden School, Southgate
Fellow of University College, London

HEINEMANN EDUCATIONAL BOOKS
LONDON

Heinemann Educational Books Ltd
LONDON EDINBURGH MELBOURNE AUCKLAND TORONTO
HONG KONG SINGAPORE KUALA LUMPUR NEW DELHI
NAIROBI JOHANNESBURG LUSAKA IBADAN
KINGSTON

ISBN 0 435 19001 6

First Published 1960
Reprinted 1961, 1962, 1963, 1966, 1967, 1970,
1974, 1975, 1976

Published by
Heinemann Educational Books Ltd
48 Charles Street, London W1X 8AH
Printed and bound in Great Britain by
Morrison & Gibb Ltd, London and Edinburgh

CONTENTS

PREFACE   *page* 1

INTRODUCTION   3

THE MERCHANT OF VENICE   23

APPENDICES:

   I   The Sources of *The Merchant of Venice*   207

  II   The Jews in Shakespeare's Day   212

 III   Shakespeare's Theatre   213

PREFACE

The aim of this edition is to encourage pupils to study the play as a play, to see it not so much as a novel or a historical narrative, but as a pattern of speech and movement creating an artistic whole. While it has been generally accepted that this approach stimulates and enlivens classroom work, it has more recently become clear that it is a most fruitful way of preparing for examinations. The recent reports issued by the Cambridge Local Examinations Syndicate call attention to this aspect in the work of both Ordinary Level and Advanced Level candidates. The following comments are taken from the Advanced Level report:

'It will be seen that the best candidates are often those who show themselves conscious of the play as a made thing—usually, but by no means, always, as a thing made for the theatre' (p. 5). Again, 'And perhaps the most misunderstood aspect of Shakespeare is the part played by theatrical convention . . .' (p. 6).

The interleaved notes, therefore, contain, in addition to a gloss, interpretations of character, dialogue and imagery, considered particularly from the point of view of a play. There are some suggestions for acting, for the most part simple pointers to avoid rigidity of interpretation and drawn up with an apron stage in mind. Some questions are interposed to provide topics for discussion or to assist in discrimination.

It is suggested that the play should be read through rapidly with as little comment as possible. On a second reading the notes should be used in detail, and appropriate sections of the Introduction might be read at the teacher's discretion.

It is hoped that this edition will enable the teacher to take his class more deeply into the play than the usual meagre allowance of time permits him to do; it is not an attempt to usurp his function.

The text is based on the First Quarto edition, 1600, but the editions of C. J. Sisson, J. Dover Wilson and Sir Arthur Quiller-Couch, and J. R. Brown have been fully consulted, and Sisson, *New Readings in Shakespeare,* has proved most valuable. A quarto reading, 'rage', II. i, 35, has been retained with Miss M. Hulme's interpretation; in III. ii, 103, 'palled' has been inserted in preference to 'pale'. Except for an omission in III. v, the text is complete. The heavy punctuation of the older school editions based on that of the Cambridge or Globe texts has been lightened. Stage directions too follow in the main those of the First Quarto which were probably Shakespeare's. The locations of scenes usually added by editors are transferred to the notes.

The interpretation of the play in the light of its morality play affinities has been partially hinted at before, particularly by Miss Hope Traver, *The Four Daughters of God,* 1907. More recently the work of G. R. Owst, *Literature and Pulpit in Medieval England,* 1933, B. Spivack, *Shakespeare and the Allegory of Evil,* 1958, and Glynne Wickham, *Early English Stages, Vol. I, 1300–1576,* 1959, has demonstrated convincingly the persistence of the morality play tradition in Elizabethan drama, and in Shakespeare in particular. For information about renaissance views of friendship and marriage I am indebted to Ruth Kelso, *Doctrine for the Lady of the Renaissance,* 1956, and particularly to L. J. Mills, *One Soul in Bodies Twain,* 1937.

I acknowledge with gratitude the stimulation I have received from the work of Miss M. C. Bradbrook, J. R. Brown, and J. W. Lever.

INTRODUCTION

I

WE do not know whether *The Merchant of Venice* was written for a special occasion, for a wedding (*A Midsummer Night's Dream, The Tempest*), or for Court festivities (*Twelfth Night*). Its first known performance was before King James at Whitehall on 10 February, 1605, and another performance was given a week later, perhaps evidence that James liked the play. This, however, was five years after a quarto edition of the play had appeared which stated on its title page, 'As it hath beene divers times acted by the Lord Chamberlaine his Servants' presumably at the Theatre or the Curtain, the two public theatres mainly used by Shakespeare's company at the time. From entries in the *Stationers' Register* and in Francis Meres' *Palladis Tamia* it is clear that these performances took place before 22 July, 1598. This together with a possible allusion in the play to the ship *Andrew*, or *St. Andrew*, captured at Cadiz, and Shakespeare's apparent knowledge of *The Orator*, a book published in 1596, show that the play was written between 30 July, 1596 and 22 July, 1598. Recently the name of the play has been discovered on a bookseller's list of 1603.

Some scholars believe that Shakespeare was urged to write the play by the continued popularity of Marlowe's play, *The Jew of Malta*, which was acted frequently from 1591 to 1596, particularly at the time of the trial and execution in 1594 of Roderigo Lopez, Queen Elizabeth's Jewish physician, and again in the first six months of 1596. *The Merchant of Venice* has phrases recalling passages in Marlowe's play, and the characters of Shylock and Jessica also show its influence. If any particular thing suggested a theme to Shakespeare, it may have been the 1596 edition of *The Faerie*

3

Queene in which Spenser made justice the 'virtue' of Book V, and in the introductory verses and the allegorical centre—the palace of Mercilla (Mercy)—he wrote on the divine and royal nature of justice and the divine quality of mercy. Mention of justice and mercy, however, is frequent in Shakespeare's plays, they were matters apparently of deep concern to Shakespeare himself.

II

Sometime in 1596-7 then, Shakespeare submitted his ideas for a play to his fellows in the company. Their approval gained, he wrote a first draft which he read over to them, inviting comments and probably making alterations and adjustments. The play was then handed to a professional scribe who made a fair copy. Probably at this stage the Master of Revels censored the play and wrote his licence to act on the last page. The book-keeper or prompter then made notes in the margin of stage properties required and directions for music or noises off, he distributed the actors' parts and rehearsals began. Two things are significant about an Elizabethan play in manuscript: the scenes were not normally marked (act division was a convention established by classical drama) and in Shakespeare's plays hardly ever is there a stage direction giving a location (there are three or four but only in his history plays). Place was unimportant, the two main entrances on the Elizabethan stage might be assumed to represent two different houses, or two different cities, Belmont and Venice, or opposing countries, but usually the spectator was expected to use his imagination; in the choruses of *Henry V* he is actually urged to do so. In performance, therefore, the play flowed on without a break; uninterrupted action on the stage was essential to preserve the link between players and audience. For the same purpose Shakespeare occasionally foreshortens time or even disregards exact chronological sequence; sometimes, as in *The Merry Wives of Windsor*, stories are started and left unfinished, but this failure to round them off passes unnoticed in the theatre.

With the intimacy permitted by the apron or open stage, place, sequence of time, costume, and even consistency of story were of less importance, so that the audience could allow themselves to be caught up into the illusion of the play. In ourselves approaching Shakespeare's plays we should bear these things very much in mind.

The company was very careful to keep the script of the play in its possession to prevent anyone from printing an unauthorized copy as had happened to several of Shakespeare's plays. However, sometime in 1600 they allowed a printer to prepare an edition using a copy of the play, possibly Shakespeare's corrected draft in his own handwriting. The First Folio edition of 1623 was based on this quarto edition of 1600. There are small inconsistencies in the play which suggest that the Clown's part has been enlarged, and that the cancelling of the masque was an alteration to the original play. Existing manuscripts of Elizabethan plays indicate that there is nothing unusual in such alterations which leave uncorrected awkwardnesses and inconsistencies.

III

The Merchant of Venice, designed to appeal to both courtier and citizen, has wide ranging variety presented with original and experimental dramatic devices. It combines an enchanted princess episode at Belmont with a folk-tale bond plot set in commercial Venice; it contains a trial, an elopement, a teasing trick over rings, and women disguised as men. Its experiments and original methods are bold and imaginative. The principal lovers are married in Act III instead of at the end of the play. Into the midst of romantic story and comic clownery Shakespeare has thrust a tragic villain, Shylock, an experiment that is unique in his comedies. Those natural enemies in Elizabethan eyes, love and friendship, are shown on the contrary as fulfilling each other in harmony. The dénouement of the bond plot with the departure of Shylock in Act IV instead of in Act V again is unusual. The use of music as a background for Lorenzo's speech, with the musicians brought actually on to the stage or on to stage level (V. i) is almost a forerunner of recitative, and together with the musical 'composition' of the earlier conversation between Lorenzo and Jessica it is an unparalleled attempt to create a mood of peace, serenity and universal harmony.

Shakespeare further emphasizes this variety by placing side by side sharply contrasting themes and characters; it is one of his favourite dramatic techniques, and he uses it boldly in this play. Portia and Antonio are both contrasted with Shylock, the New Law with the Old Law, the marriage bond with the flesh bond, love with hatred, deceptive appearances with inner truth, generosity with miserliness.

For good measure he adds discussions or comments on friendship, usury, melancholy, music, national characteristics, and that perennial, light-hearted topic, the oddity of a young Englishman's clothes. There is a song, there is instrumental music, and there is a brilliant display of pageantry at Belmont and in Venice, perhaps the most colourful in any of Shakespeare's comedies.

Such a mixture was not devised for idle amusement only, or to allow the spectators to escape into a world of romance and comic interludes; it sets up values and judgements of good and evil, the proclaimed purpose of Elizabethan literature in general. *The Merchant of Venice* contains themes of deep moral and social concern presented parable-wise in action, or in discussion or in a soliloquy—the relationship of justice and mercy, sacrifice, the reconciliation of love and friendship, the Old Testament doctrine and the New Testament teaching, Christian charity in practice. Some scholars consider that each of Shakespeare's plays has one theme or governing moral idea which pervades and controls the play and to which all other themes contribute. The theme of love and friendship has been suggested for *The Merchant of Venice*, and this theme receives expanded treatment later (p. 9) in order to bring out what interpretation the Elizabethans put on these two ideas. The opposition of justice and mercy in the trial scene, viewed in the light of the allegory of the Four Daughters of God, has also been proposed. This judgement theme is shown later (p. 11) to permeate the whole play. The falsity of appearances besides the truth of reality which is openly stated in Bassanio's soliloquy over the caskets and implicit in the discussion over usury (I. iii, 63–91) and in Shylock's pretence of friendship (I. iii, 133–166) is another possibility. J. R. Brown (*Shakespeare and his Comedies*, pp. 45–75) has suggested love's wealth or the prosperity and happiness of mind that spring from giving rather than from taking. A further suggestion is that love and friendship, above the false show of material things, is prepared to make an entire sacrifice, and in so doing is shown to be a reflection in human terms of the Christian Redemption.

The characters serving different dramatic purposes are variously presented. Shylock is revealed by soliloquy and in dialogue; Portia and Antonio are revealed by the descriptions of others as well as in dialogue; Bassanio reveals himself almost entirely in dialogue. Generally in a comedy the lesser characters 'speak for themselves'. However they reveal themselves, Shakespeare's genius gives them vivid human touches; the greater figures like Shylock and Hamlet engage our sympathies so deeply that we are often deceived into thinking of them as if they had a life outside the play. The tradition of the stage produced a number of stock characters who invariably behave like puppets in the same limited way. When Shakespeare uses one of them, Launcelot Gobbo, for example, he invests the character with a fresh, life-like appearance, and occasionally refers to its ancestry to score a dramatic point. A minor character such as Launcelot, Nerissa, or Horatio (*Hamlet*) may change function to meet the dramatic needs of the plot. Salerio, Solanio and Gratiano are not only Antonio's friends, they act as a chorus in making the kind of comment on affairs expected from an onlooker. Occasionally characters represent a quality or state. Time (*The Winter's Tale*) and

Rumour (*Henry IV*, Part II) indicate their purpose by their name, Adam (*As You Like It*) and Caliban (*The Tempest*) give a less obvious indication of the qualities they represent. In *The Merchant of Venice* Morocco and Arragon are allegorical figures personifying fleshly desire and pride; this being so, is Bassanio to be seen in a similar way? A number of characters in Shakespeare's tragedies, while they are not personifications in this way, are clearly involved in moral qualities, states or ideas; this is also true of some characters in his comedies. At times their human qualities are uppermost; at other times they speak as if they were mouthpieces of some quality. Is Shylock an injured father, the Old Law, the Devil, or Justice? Is Portia an enchanted princess, Wisdom, Mercy, or a quick-witted Elizabethan? Is Antonio a faithful friend or Mankind? All this fits in with the Elizabethans' habit of moralizing, of thinking in terms of allegory, and with their capacity for seeing multiple meanings in one thing.

Shakespeare characteristically says more than one thing at a time, sometimes his characters play as it were more than one part, and his plots tell more than one story. This makes interpretation of a play such as *The Merchant of Venice* very difficult. Succeeding ages have selected some aspects of character or theme as significant of the whole at the expense of other aspects, or have developed entirely new beliefs and judgements. Our views on usury, Jews, Christianity, and friendship are different from those Shakespeare expresses in the play. We find it impossible to approve the open Elizabethan contempt for the Jew, and the militant Christianity which generously and logically offers Shylock salvation by compelling him to become a Christian. The changing presentation of Shylock on later stages is a convenient illustration.

Originally, if a much altered eighteenth-century version of the play is any guide, Shylock was a comic character, a figure of derision and mockery. The extant verses which state that the part of Shylock was played by Richard Burbage, the chief actor of Shakespeare's company, in a red-haired wig are perhaps a forgery. Later Shylock was played by Macklin as so grotesque, sinister, and ferocious a villain that George II spent a sleepless night after attending a performance. Then he was played as a much injured man, an outraged father who moved his audience to pity and tears over his wrongs. Later still he was presented as an Old Testament prophet strong in his faith. Recently it has even been hinted that he is Shakespeare's view of a capitalist!

Similarly, even within a few years of this century the estimates of Bassanio's character have touched extremes. One view classes him as a 'waster, a rotter or both'; another thinks that 'firmly handled, he might even ripen into a good husband'; while another, referring his behaviour to the courtesy books of the period, describes him as an 'ideal lover'.

Because of Shakespeare's methods and the changes in intellectual opinion and social custom, much in his plays is likely to be meaningless or imperfect to our minds unless some attempt is made to recover even a little of the Elizabethan attitude of mind and scope of their knowledge. To assist in this, one theme from the play is described below as an Elizabethan courtier might regard it, and a second theme is treated in the light of a morality play tradition. The main characters, it will be noted, are the same in both, and thus have a double function.

IV

The love versus friendship theme was deeply felt and closely debated in the Renaissance. It appeared in differing story forms; in some of which one of the friends was killed, but the version which Shakespeare adopted in *All's Well* and *The Merchant of Venice* placed the claims of friendship above those of love between man and woman.

The friendship between Antonio and Bassanio is of this profound nature. Antonio, the more important figure, unhesitatingly shares his wealth with Bassanio in spite of the latter's confession of his shortcomings. In this he enhances his own character by behaving in correct Christian charity and as the complete friend. His attitude towards Shylock is partly dictated by the accepted belief that usury and friendship were enemies, the former destructive of the latter. To an audience unaware of the plot Antonio's sadness and Shylock's declared hatred may well raise fears after the bond has been sealed that Antonio may have to sacrifice his life. His offer is the greater since, according to a medieval belief, he put himself like Christ into the power of Jewry. In their conversation Antonio declares the opposition between usury and friendship, and Shylock, seizing his chance baits his trap with an offer of friendship. Antonio, who represents friendship, is unable in his melancholy state to see the deception of an offer made in the name of friendship.

When the news of Antonio's misfortune reaches Belmont, Bassanio with fine integrity confesses the debt he owes to Antonio, which, because of the honourable course expected of him as a friend, may well destroy his new happiness. His divided loyalties are reconciled by the wisdom of Portia who perceives that true love is achieved only by preserving friendship. Her sacrifice is considerable. As man and wife she and Bassanio are 'one flesh', but as friends Bassanio and Antonio are 'one soul in bodies twain', and she accepts the superiority of that claim as her conversation with Lorenzo (III. iv) makes clear.

Bassanio's offer of his life in the trial scene is seriously meant, and not the 'manifest lie' which one critic, mistaking the stage for reality, has suggested. Similarly, his offer to renounce his wife to save his friend is a serious offer although Shakespeare quickly turns it to jest with Portia's comment.

It has been suggested that Antonio's voluntary sharing of his wealth with Bassanio is precisely balanced—to the delight of an Elizabethan audience—by the retribution that befalls Shylock. He, the pretended friend, is ordered to share his wealth with Antonio, his bond-brother, and so carry out the accepted doctrine that friends should share their goods.

The ring episode is another bond pledge. Bassanio again allows the request of his friend to overrule his wife's wishes, that is he places friendship above love. Again Bassanio confesses what happened, and this time Antonio makes a deeper sacrifice, he offers to pledge his soul that Bassanio will prove true; in other words he acknowledges Portia's claim to Bassanio and offers her that which he shares with Bassanio, 'one soul in bodies twain'. The resolving of love and friendship in harmony symbolized by the music of Act V is complete.

V

While the influence of the morality theme, the Four Daughters of God (Appendix I), cannot be precisely ascribed to any one source, its general implications are too apt to ignore, particularly in view of the numerous Biblical allusions in the play. Antonio then represents Mankind, the somewhat passive central figure of the play; Shylock represents the Devil, or, perhaps, in the trial scene Justice; Portia represents Wisdom or Mercy. A subsidiary part of the allegory is represented by Morocco, worldly desire; Arragon, intellectual pride; and Bassanio, understanding, in their quest for Portia.

Antonio's sadness may be quite simply the misery of fallen mankind. The opening of the morality play, the *Castle of Perseverance*, based on the Four Daughters theme, describes similarly the sad state of man after the Fall. Moreover, Antonio's friends treat him as a sinner: Solanio and Salerio preach him in effect a sermon (I. i, 8–40) on the misery and anxiety that the possession of wealth causes, particularly to merchants—a commonplace of moral writings and pulpit. Then the irreverent Gratiano, unexpectedly serious-minded, adds another homily on hypocrisy (I. i, 88–99) reminiscent of *St. Matthew*, VI. 16. Later, Antonio refers to himself as a 'tainted wether ... meetest for death', which suggests that he has become aware of his sinful condition. His conduct at first is in strict Christian friendship, for he not only shares his wealth freely with Bassanio, but he also forgives him his debts. All this is to enhance his dramatic standing, for he is more important to the play than Bassanio.

Shylock's soliloquy of hatred (I. iii, 35–46) follows the tradition of the Vice in the morality plays who likewise declared his hatred of virtue and his intention to overthrow it or mankind by lying and deceit. That Shylock is conceived as the Devil or sib to him, is amply supported by references in the text (I. iii, 93; II. ii, 19–20, 22; II. iii, 2; III. i, 17–18, 27), and his constant reference to beasts is a characteristic devilish association. He traps Antonio, one might say he tempts him (I. iii, 92), by blandly assuming that Antonio's attitude towards him has been hostile and lacking in friendliness. Antonio is deceived by the offer of friendship and his own sense of security.

Launcelot's imaginary dialogue with his good angel and a fiend, (II. ii, 1–26), a parody of a morality play theme, acts as an inverted image of the main theme in this play; it sets the morality play issue clearly before the audience. Both he and Jessica escape from 'hell' (II. iii, 2), and while he, like all clowns, is timeless, indestructible and amoral (his new livery however may signify conversion as it does in the morality play *Magnificence*), Jessica has to be sealed of the Christian faith, and Shakespeare firmly establishes this in a scene (III. v) that has been condemned as dramatically useless.

The resemblances in the trial scene are apparent: the belated appearance of the disguised Portia, unlike the female lawyer's appearance in the other sources, her apparent siding with the claimant, the praise of her wisdom, the scales, the mercy-speech which goes far beyond the appeal to mercy by the Judge in *Zelauto* (Appendix I), and Shylock's departure in disgrace. Portia's speech with its profound appeal and challenge leads directly to the turning point in the trial, Shylock's reply, 'My deeds upon my head'. These words recall the cry of the Jews demanding the death of Christ, they are also a challenge to nemesis, and in Elizabethan eyes to claim responsibility for one's deeds was presumptuously to claim equality with God—and that was Satan's sin. The immediate granting of mercy to Shylock by sparing his life, his compulsory conversion which, however repugnant we may find it, offers him the greatest gift a Christian could bestow, the possibility of salvation, a share in the Kingdom of Heaven, a share, as a friend, in spiritual wealth—all this is closely allied to the trend of thought, though nothing of the kind has been traced to any source story.

While Shakespeare may have followed his main source, *Il Pecorone*, in giving Portia so much freedom in court, it is odd that the form of the trial, so unlike any legal process, should have been offered to the legally knowledgeable Elizabethans. If its presentation was intended to be in part allegorical, such accuracy would not have been necessary or even desirable.

If it is accepted that an allegorical vein exists in the play, and that the music of Act V. 1 represents the harmony and peace of Belmont and of reconciliation parallel with the celestial songs after the reconciliation of the Four Daughters, may it not also include the improbable journeyings of Antonio's ships? The comparison of a ship's voyage with the life of man was a popular one (see Owst, *Literature and Pulpit*, pp. 68–74). Twice the comparison is made in the play: Salerio portrays Antonio's argosies 'with portly sail, Like signiors and rich burghers on the flood' (I. i, 9–10), and Gratiano elaborates the comparison by joining to it the parable of the Prodigal Son (II. vi, 14–19). Shakespeare could have committed Antonio's wealth to one ship as in his source, but he strains belief when all Antonio's ships, trading in many parts of the world, are all reported lost, and even more so when Portia reports that three are safe but refuses to offer any explanation (V. i, 275–9). Are these very improbabilities intended to indicate that Antonio's argosies are a symbol of his own life, that the ship of Mankind has come safely into harbourage at Belmont?

This isolating of themes and characters for examination cannot fully represent their part when merged in the living play. Its action moves with varying intensity in the fields of romance, comedy, and allegory, or allegory may give way to conventional romance and comedy or to everyday realism. The improbabilities and inconsequences to which attention has often been drawn are thus seen not as blemishes but resolving themselves as the natural consequences of such variable movement. In short the variety, the contrasts, the shifting modes of presentation, together with its Christian themes of love, sacrifice, and judgement, would have made it an admirable choice for a performance at Court on, say, the feast of Corpus Christi.

VI

The stage conditions described in Appendix III determined to a large extent the shape of the plays, their dramatic devices, their methods and conventions.

The general lack of scenery gave the dramatist freedom to shift the scene of his play as often as he liked (*Antony and Cleopatra* has thirteen scenes in Act III), to change the scene unannounced while the actors remained on the stage (*Twelfth Night*, III. iv, begins in Olivia's orchard and ends in the street), or, where knowledge of locality was not necessary for the understanding of the plot, to place it nowhere in particular (is II. v, inside or outside Shylock's house?). The precise locating of every scene would distract attention from the plot; the scene is where the actors are. Such imprecision coupled with the rapid two-hour flow of the play, uninterrupted by breaks for scene or costume changes, helped to maintain the dramatic spell.

There was a similar freedom in the treatment of time. Inevitably some scenes overlapped, but Shakespeare placed scenes out of their chronological order, he foreshortened time, or sometimes he merely confused it. How long did Bassanio's voyage and wooing take? (See I. iii, 2; III. ii, 317–18). The concern is not with the orderly sequence of events in real life but with the illusion of time in a play. Occasionally the passage of time is mentioned, and its touch of realism adds a depth to the play, but it may not fit in with indications of time given elsewhere in the play. Try to work out a satisfactory time-plan for *The Merchant of Venice*; there are three unsatisfactory ones already in print.

Shakespeare, however, considered it important to mark chronological order for dramatic reasons in the choruses of *Henry V* to simulate the fashion of an epic poem, and in the speech of Time in *The Winter's Tale* to mark the balance of fathers with children, the court with the country, jealous intrigue with love and friendship.

The plays at the Globe took place in the afternoon and daytime was assumed in their action. Night was mentioned directly or by reference to torches, candles, or tapers, etc., if the action demanded it, as in *A Midsummer Night's Dream*, and in *Julius Caesar*, or, as in *Macbeth*, to help create an atmosphere of horror and evil.

An important convention was the practice of the soliloquy and the aside. The jutting out of the stage into the middle of the theatre floor brought the actors who were well forward nearer to the bulk of the audience than to actors at the rear of the stage. It had long been established that character and motives were announced directly, the audience was not left to guess what was going on in a character's mind. It was a simple matter, therefore, for an actor to come forward out of earshot of the others on the stage and reveal confidentially to the audience his character, his motives and his intentions. In this way Shylock and Richard III declared their villainy, Prince Hal his intention to give up his bad companions, Olivia her love for Viola and Launcelot the struggle with his conscience. This device linked actor and audience intimately: the spectators shared in the play, they had a god-like knowledge of the hearts of the characters, and the two things increased their feelings of tension and suspense and the moments of dramatic irony. The aside, a brief pointed remark, is often ironic, or it may give the audience a kind of nudge to remind them of some matter. It too sustains the sense of intimacy between actor and audience.

The use of boys for female parts made easy the disguising of the heroine in male dress, and the comedy, vivacity and cross-purposes that surround Viola, Rosalind and Imogen show that Shakespeare approved of it. Such a device seems clumsy and improbable to us. It is a commonplace in the romantic stories of Shakespeare's time, and one of Elizabeth I's maids of honour wore the garments of a page to visit her lover, so that the costume may have been an effective disguise. In any case the capacity for make-believe among the audience was sufficient for them to accept any disguising however absurd (e.g. Falstaff as Mother Prat, *Merry Wives*, IV. ii, 188) as impenetrable.

The ornate stage, the magnificent costumes, the royal and noble characters produced an element of formal pageantry in the performance of the plays. Gesture and stage business were formal, dignified and restricted, and the emphasis was placed on the delivery of the speeches. To an audience accustomed to the impressive oratory of preachers at St. Paul's Cross, to sustained and eloquent speaking by its notabilities trained in rhetoric, the words of a play were particularly important. A well-spoken passage of rich word-painting for example reporting some event that had happened off stage was rousing and satisfying. It was a kind of pageantry in speech or as a Jacobean writer put it, 'an ampullous and scenicall pomp' of words.

VII

The impact of dialogue was enhanced by its traditional verse form; it gave to the major characters an impressive grandeur, a stature larger than life. In Shakespeare's plays its range, power and flexibility are truly astounding, and he contrasts it from time to time with passages of prose almost as varied in style and form.

Shakespeare's verse is infinitely varied. He uses heroic couplets to form a stately narrative verse in *Richard II*, or two speakers can each speak a line of a couplet, the second speaker making a comment on the first (*A Midsummer Night's Dream*, I. i, 196-201). A few couplets appearing in blank verse may mark an intense emotion; a single couplet may mark a wise or significant saying, or an important exit. Couplets can impart a sense of finality, of steps taken from which there can be no turning back. Couplets of shorter lines, however, are often mocking jingles (*The Merchant of Venice*, I. i, 111–2) though they too can be impressively final (*A Midsummer Night's Dream*, V. i, 404 ff.).

In early plays such as *Love's Labour's Lost* and *Romeo and Juliet* Shakespeare used elaborate rhyme patterns. The first words Romeo and Juliet speak to each other form the pattern of a sonnet. Such patterns employed with elaborate figures of speech are a sign of the depth and sincerity of the speakers' feelings. We are inclined to regard them as artificial and insincere, but to an Elizabethan they truly reflected the strength and complexity of the emotion described.

Shakespeare's blank verse can be elaborate, enriched with swiftly following metaphors, with similes and other figures of speech or tricks of style, and with mythological allusions; it can be plain and direct; or it can become exaggerated and violent in language in the description of warfare, in frenzied appeals to the heavens, and in boasting. Its rhythms can march with regular beat, or, particularly in later plays like *King Lear* and *Antony and Cleopatra*, the rhythms are infinitely varied to achieve the most subtle effects. The characters use the kind of blank verse appropriate to the dramatic moment and not necessarily the kind consistent with what is known of them in the play. Thus in *Macbeth* it is worth thinking over why the murderers of Banquo speak in blank verse. Again, in the same play why should the doctor watching Lady Macbeth suddenly change from prose to blank verse after Lady Macbeth had returned to bed?

Prose is normally used by comic or low characters as befitting their rank, and by contrast with the verse spoken by the courtiers. It can present the stumbling conversation of a Dogberry or Verges, the chop-logic of Feste and Touchstone, the wit and expressiveness of Falstaff illuminated by vivid similes, and the power and passion of Shylock. Shakespeare's concern was always with dramatic effect. After Caesar's murder, Shakespeare made Brutus, who elsewhere spoke blank verse, utter his flat, uninspired speech to the mob in prose as a sharp contrast to the full power of the blank verse speech he gave Antony. Why did Shakespeare make Shylock speak in blank verse, I. iii, 35–170, but in prose I. iii, 1–33? Why was prose used in I. ii? Elsewhere Portia speaks in blank verse.

It is sometimes very difficult to understand why Shakespeare changes the dialogue from verse to prose or from one style of blank verse to another. Occasionally the changes may be due to cuts, alterations or additions made to the original play, but in general the variations are deliberately designed to achieve some dramatic effect. They should not, therefore, be overlooked or lightly dismissed in your study of the play.

VIII

The nature of the vocabulary, images and allusions gives a colouring to the play as a whole and to individual characters. Words and images connected with merchandise and wealth are common in the Venetian scenes, but it is surprising to find such words frequently used in III. ii in the speeches of Portia and Bassanio. J. R. Brown (*Shakespeare and his Comedies*, pp. 64–9) points out that in this play and in *Romeo and Juliet* and the *Sonnets* Shakespeare regards love as a kind of usury which lovers practise for the joy of giving. On the other hand Shylock is frequently likened directly and indirectly to a devil, and accordingly and appropriately his speeches make reference to beasts: beefs, muttons, goats, ewes, rams, curs, snail, drone, wildcat, rat, serpent, dog, and he is likened to a wolf by Gratiano.

There are many detailed analyses of Shakespeare's thought and imagery; one characteristic of his style may be mentioned, what has been called the 'streaminess' of his thought. This is not the deliberate sustaining of an image of thought, as that of the rack (III. ii, 25–37), but an illustration is provided by the words 'draw it out in length' in l. 23, which perhaps unconsciously prompted the 'rack' image. This apparently unconscious way in which one idea is linked with, or gives rise to, the next reveals some delightful associations of thought. See III. ii, 176–84, speaks—oration—buzzing—expressed; I. i, 29, burial—church; II. ix, 46–8, peasantry gleaned seed chaff, and various linkings in III. ii, 75–82.

It is a commonplace that Shakespeare's plays abound in allusions to classical myths and stories, particularly those derived from Ovid's poems. Usually Shakespeare puts these allusions in the mouths of the characters in his comedies who figure in the romantic theme of the plays. In *The Merchant of Venice* Bassanio, Portia, Morocco, Lorenzo, and Jessica all make use of them as befitting their parts. Is it in keeping with Antonio's part that he makes no such reference at all? It is surely significant that Shylock does not refer to the courtly world of classical culture. On the other hand Shakespeare's fools indulge in a parade of mock-learning, and Launcelot is no exception with his allusions to the Fates and to Scylla and Charybdis.

In Shakespeare's early comedies generally, images or references derived from the New Testament, relating among other things to justice, mercy, redemption, and atonement are more prevalent than in the plays of his contemporaries. In this play there are a number of direct references, and, even more than usual, lines of thought which echo passages in the Epistles to the *Romans, Galatians* and *Corinthians*. Allowing for some phrases that may have been used without knowledge of their biblical associations, there remain sufficient parallels to be of some importance in considering the interpretation of the play as a whole.

IX

Elizabethan schooling provided training in rhetoric, that is the art of using words to persuade, to emphasize, and to display eloquence and wit. A most complex system of large numbers of figures of speech, devices of style and processes of thought had been formulated, and Shakespeare makes extensive use of them. While for the most part it is enough to be aware that Shakespeare's apparent spontaneous ease in writing arises from a strict training in rhetoric, a few devices in *The Merchant of Venice* should be noticed.

A topic for discussion was ideally arranged in three parts, so Lorenzo describes Jessica as wise, fair, and true with a comment on each (II. vi, 53–6) and Portia is 'richly left', and 'fair' and 'of wondrous virtues'.

Devices such as the turning round of a sentence (I. ii, 93), the turning of an opponent's argument which is accepted against him (Portia's invitation to Shylock to take the pound of flesh), the partition of a subject (III. i, 52–9), malapropisms, the introduction of proverbs are all fairly commonplace.

The construction of Shylock's argument, IV. i, 35–62; 89–103, is extremely careful. It introduces the subject of Shylock's claim, his reason, similar instances and their application to the present situation; then in ll. 89–103 he insists on his right, cites a parallel and applies it to his own case and concludes with a demand for justice. Similarly Bassanio's debate with himself about ornament and false appearances III. ii, 73–102, repays close examination.

To an Elizabethan audience a good deal of the fun caused by Launcelot was his use of mock learning and the verbal confusions he falls into. His learned references to the Sisters Three, the deliciously inappropriate identification of Jessica's parents with Scylla and Charybdis, and his playing with a 'tricksy word' are in a sense a parody of rhetorical devices.

An effort of imagination is required if we are to appreciate the importance and value of the puns that Shakespeare uses so frequently. What has been regarded in recent times as the lowest form of wit, was, as Kellett has shown, used with telling force by Isaiah and St. Paul and by the Greek dramatists. Among the

Elizabethans it was an accepted means of showing intellectual brilliance and verbal dexterity. Shakespeare enlarges its scope: it may produce a simple jest or emphasize a point (Lady Macbeth's

> I'll gild the faces of the grooms withall
> For it *must seem their guilt*

is horrifyingly emphatic, it is not hysterical.)

It may sharpen the irony of an aside 'A little more than kin and less than kind'; it may be a flash of bitter insight (in *Romeo and Juliet*, the gay Mercutio mortally wounded says, 'Ask for me to-morrow, and you shall find me a grave man'); and it may be employed in an exchange of witticisms.

Sometimes Shakespeare uses the two meanings of a word simultaneously, or one meaning will give way to another as the sentence proceeds ('tossing', I. i, 8), sometimes the word is repeated bearing a second meaning, or sometimes a word may have the meaning of a word of similar sound imposed upon it (in *Love's Labour's Lost* 'haud credo' is confused with 'ow'd grey doe', and in *As You Like It* 'goats' with 'Goths').

THE MERCHANT
OF VENICE

CHARACTERS

THE DUKE OF VENICE
THE PRINCE OF MOROCCO ⎫
THE PRINCE OF ARRAGON ⎭ suitors to Portia
ANTONIO, a Merchant of Venice
BASSANIO, his friend, suitor to Portia
SOLANIO ⎫
SALERIO ⎬ friends to Antonio and Bassanio
GRATIANO ⎭
LORENZO, in love with Jessica
SHYLOCK, a rich Jew
TUBAL, a Jew, his friend
LAUNCELOT GOBBO, a clown, servant to Shylock
OLD GOBBO, father to Launcelot
LEONARDO, servant to Bassanio
BALTHASAR ⎫
STEPHANO ⎭ servants to Portia

PORTIA, an heiress
NERISSA, her waiting-woman
JESSICA, daughter to Shylock

Magnificoes of Venice, Officers of the Court of Justice, Gaoler, Musicians, Servants, and other Attendants

SCENE: *Venice, and Portia's house at Belmont*

Venice

Is this an indoor or outdoor scene? Are any properties required?

Antonio's entrance with his friends should help to show his mood. Does he lean on the others, or is he trying to move away from their persistent questioning? Should his dress be disordered?

1 *In . . . sad.* Assume that this is an emphatic reply to his friend's questions.

3, 4 *caught, found, came by, stuff, born.* Possibly Antonio should give the impression that he is repeating words used by Salerio and Solanio.

5 *I . . . learn,* I do not know. The incomplete line may indicate a pause before Antonio admits the overwhelming nature of his sadness.

Many attempts have been made to account for Antonio's sadness: anxiety about the safety of his ships; the coming departure and possible loss in marriage of Bassanio; that he is a Christian aware of his sinfulness; that he is filled with nameless foreboding of evil; that a serious character is necessary for a merchant and for one who is about to offer his life for his friend; that in his moodiness he is the likelier to fall into Shylock's trap; that it is inexplicable and serves merely to distinguish him from his friends. Which of these has the most dramatic value? Remember that you should not invent a life for Antonio outside the play.

7 Is Antonio irritated, impatient, petulant, weary, tired, anxious, cynical, bored, amused at himself, annoyed with himself, tortured in mind?

8 *tossing,* (*a*) troubled, tormented (in mind), (*b*) pitching to and fro (on the ocean). The second meaning is involved when the word 'ocean' is spoken.

9 *There.* Perhaps an airy gesture as in imagination he pictures the magnificent argosies.
   argosies, large merchant ships (from 'Arragosa', modern Ragusa, an Italian port).
   portly, (*a*) swelling, corpulent (like 'rich burghers', l. 10), (*b*) majestic (like 'pageants', l. 11).

ACT ONE

SCENE ONE

Enter ANTONIO, SALERIO, *and* SOLANIO

ANTONIO: In sooth I know not why I am so sad.
  It wearies me, you say it wearies you;
  But how I caught it, found it, or came by it,
  What stuff 'tis made of, whereof it is born,
  I am to learn.
  And such a want-wit sadness makes of me,
  That I have much ado to know myself.
SALERIO: Your mind is tossing on the ocean,
  There, where your argosies with portly sail,

10   *flood*, sea.

11   *pageants*, moveable structures shaped like ships, castles, etc., that were drawn as spectacles about the streets on festive occasions.

12   *overpeer*, look down on (in both senses). A pun on 'peer' (of the realm) has been suggested.
       petty traffickers, small trading ships.

13   *curtsy*, (*a*) respectfully bow the knee, (*b*) bob up and down in the waves.

14   Salerio identifies Antonio as the merchant of the play by describing his very wealthy trading vessels which, he implies, are a source of great anxiety.

       The words 'argosies', 'portly', 'signiors', 'rich burghers', 'pageants', 'traffickers', 'curtsy', 'reverence' give the impression of a wealthy, well-ordered, maritime society.

       Does Solanio interrupt Salerio? Has Salerio lost the thread of his speech in the picture he is creating?

15   *venture*, a trading enterprise in which the merchants took the chance of losing their money or of obtaining a profit.
       forth, sent out.

16   *affections*, feelings.

17   *hopes*, i.e. his ships.
       still, continually.

18   *Plucking . . . wind*, throwing blades of grass into the air to tell from which direction the wind blows. *sits*, blows from.

19   *roads*, anchorages—where ships 'ride' at anchor.

22   Solanio's words describe another aspect of trading—navigation.

23   *blow . . . ague*. Some winds, notably the south wind, were thought to bring diseases. *ague*, (*a*) fever marked by shivering, (*b*) a fit of shivering with fear, a 'fever of anxiety'.

22–40   Should any gestures or miming be used to emphasize the far-fetched statements in this speech or not?

26   *flats*, stretches of flat sand in shallow water.

27   *Andrew*. This may refer to *St. Andrew*, a Spanish galleon, captured at Cadiz in July 1596.
       docked, embedded.

28   *vailing*, lowering. *high-top*, topsail, or the platform from which the topsail was handled.

       The mainmast is broken and lies with its top on the sand as if bowing with submission and grief at the burial of the ship.

29–31   *church . . . rocks*. An extreme suggestion since the church is a symbol of safety and security.

Like signiors and rich burghers on the flood, 10
Or as it were the pageants of the sea,
Do overpeer the petty traffickers
That curtsy to them, do them reverence,
As they fly by them with their woven wings.

SOLANIO: Believe me sir, had I such venture forth,
The better part of my affections would
Be with my hopes abroad. I should be still
Plucking the grass to know where sits the wind,
Peering in maps for ports and piers and roads;
And every object that might make me fear 20
Misfortune to my ventures, out of doubt
Would make me sad.

SALERIO: My wind, cooling my broth,
Would blow me to an ague when I thought
What harm a wind too great might do at sea.
I should not see the sandy hour-glass run,
But I should think of shallows and of flats,
And see my wealthy Andrew docked in sand,
Vailing her high-top lower than her ribs
To kiss her burial. Should I go to church
And see the holy edifice of stone, 30
And not bethink me straight of dangerous rocks,

32   *gentle*, noble.

35–6   *but . . . nothing*, at one moment carrying all this valuable cargo, at the next moment it is worthless.

38   *such . . . bechanced*, if such a thing happened it.

39   *But . . . me*. Was Antonio about to protest?

40   Solanio and Salerio are earnestly trying to help Antonio. Tactfully assuming their inferiority to the 'royal' merchant, Antonio, they admit that under the strain of his responsibilities they would agitatedly reveal their anxiety. Salerio, taking up Solanio's point (ll. 20–2), describes far-fetched associations which would torment him with fears, hoping that their half humorous extravagance will move Antonio to laughter, and thus will dispel his sadness.

42   *bottom*, ship.

44   *Upon*, dependent on.

47, 49   *say . . . say*. These should carry some emphasis.

47–8   *sad . . . merry*. A popular saying.

50   *two-headed Janus*. The Roman god of doors. He was represented with two heads facing opposite ways, one face was frowning, the other was smiling. Solanio means that Janus was himself a strange fellow with opposing moods in the same body.

52   *peep . . . eyes*, i.e. their eyes are screwed up with laughter.

52–6   Does Solanio mimic these sounds or appearances to try to make Antonio laugh? Is Antonio bored, amused, irritated, joyful, unmoved, at all this?

53–6   *laugh . . . laughable*, laugh with foolish screeches at the melancholy sound of the bagpipes, and others who will remain with a sour face even though so grave a person as Nestor takes his oath that the joke is funny.

53   *parrots*. Foolish birds in popular opinion.
        bagpiper, bagpipes.

54   *other*. Formerly plural.
        aspect. Stress the second syllable.

Which touching but my gentle vessel's side
Would scatter all her spices on the stream,
Enrobe the roaring waters with my silks,
And in a word, but even now worth this,
And now worth nothing? Shall I have the thought
To think on this, and shall I lack the thought
That such a thing bechanced would make me sad?
But tell not me, I know Antonio
Is sad to think upon his merchandise.   40

ANTONIO: Believe me no, I thank my fortune for it,
My ventures are not in one bottom trusted,
Nor to one place; nor is my whole estate
Upon the fortune of this present year.
Therefore my merchandise makes me not sad.

SALERIO: Why then you are in love.

ANTONIO: Fie, fie!

BOLANIO: Not in love neither: then let us say you are sad,
Because you are not merry; and 'twere as easy
For you to laugh and leap and say you are merry
Because you are not sad. Now by two-headed Janus,   50
Nature hath framed strange fellows in her time:
Some that will evermore peep through their eyes
And laugh like parrots at a bagpiper;
And other of such vinegar aspect

56   *Nestor.* One of the Greek leaders at the siege of Troy, noted for his wisdom and his extreme old age.

How would you distinguish Solanio from Salerio? Which words are appropriate: mincing, blunt, practical, direct, affected, abrupt, thin-voiced, foppish, dandyish, plain, squeamish?

57   *most noble kinsman.* Bassanio and Antonio are clearly of higher social standing than the others. No other mention is made of this relationship.

61   *prevented,* forestalled.

62   *worth.* Antonio courteously sets aside Salerio's self-humbling comparison and emphasizes 'Your worth'. 'You are a worthy friend and accordingly dear to me'.

66   *laugh,* i.e. have a merry meeting.

67   *you . . . strange,* you are becoming complete strangers.

68   *We'll . . . yours,* we will be free to meet you whenever you are ready.

73-6   *you . . . changed.* Gratiano and Lorenzo have not previously noticed Antonio's sadness. They are shocked and delay their departure.

74   *respect . . . world,* regard to worldly matters.

75   *They . . . care.* Originally a version of *St. Mark,* viii. 36: 'For what shall it profit a man if he shall gain the whole world and lose his own soul' or *St. Matthew,* xvi. 25: 'Whosoever will save his life shall lose it'.

77-8   *I hold . . . part.* A comparison which Shakespeare mentions elsewhere, particularly, 'All the world's a stage' *As You Like It,* II. vii, 139-66.

That they'll not show their teeth in way of smile
Though Nestor swear the jest be laughable.

Enter BASSANIO, LORENZO, *and* GRATIANO

Here comes Bassanio your most noble kinsman,
   Gratiano, and Lorenzo. Fare ye well,
   We leave you now with better company.
SALERIO: I would have stayed till I had made you merry,   60
   If worthier friends had not prevented me.
ANTONIO: Your worth is very dear in my regard.
   I take it your own business calls on you,
   And you embrace th'occasion to depart.
SALERIO: Good morrow my good lords.
BASSANIO: Good signiors both when shall we laugh? say, when?
   You grow exceeding strange. Must it be so?
SALERIO: We'll make our leisures to attend on yours.
                   [Exeunt Salerio and Solanio
LORENZO: My Lord Bassanio, since you have found Antonio,
   We two will leave you, but at dinner-time   70
   I pray you have in mind where we must meet.
BASSANIO: I will not fail you.
GRATIANO: You look not well Signior Antonio,
   You have too much respect upon the world.
   They lose it that do buy it with much care;
   Believe me you are marvellously changed.
ANTONIO: I hold the world but as the world, Gratiano,
   A stage where every man must play a part,
   And mine a sad one.

79–   Which words best fit Antonio's mood in this speech: patient,
104   long-suffering, spiritless, humble, passive, dignified, mournful?

Gratiano takes up Antonio's reference to playing a part; the theme of acting underlies his speech. He assumes that Antonio's melancholy is a fashionable pose (common among the Elizabethan gallants). For himself he would play the Fool's part and live a merry riotous life; the sober, gloomy, frigid life he regards as unnatural for a warm blooded man. Then, protesting that it is only his love for Antonio that makes him speak in a reproving way, he describes those who play the part of silent, straight-faced, arrogant hypocrites in order to gain a reputation for wisdom and great intelligence when their stupid speech would drive their hearers to call them fools and so suffer damnation. He begs Antonio not to put on a melancholy appearance to gain a reputation for wisdom only among credulous people.

Gratiano is half serious, half jesting in describing the extremes of riot and hypocritical moroseness. There is the satirical hint of an arrogant, bigoted Puritan preacher who breaks off his sermon to go to his dinner, and a touch of mock pulpit style with quotations from the Bible. This fantastic creature, he implies, is what Antonio may become, if he allows his melancholy to go any further.

79   *play . . . fool, (a)* behave foolishly, make merry, *(b)* play the part of the Fool on the stage.

80   *old,* in old age.

82   *heart . . . groans.* Sighs and groans were believed to draw drops of blood from the heart and even to bring about death.

84   *sit . . . alabaster,* i.e. sit like the effigy of his grandfather carved in cold alabaster on a monument in church.

85   *Sleep . . . wakes,* falls asleep when he should stay awake for merry-making or for a vigil, or, more asleep than awake.

86   *peevish,* depressed, morose. Depression of mind is associated with jaundice.

88   *sort,* number.

89   *cream . . . pond,* fixed, unmoving yellow and green skin.
      cream, become congealed. *mantle,* become covered with green weed.
      Possibly 'cream' and 'mantle' carry on the association of yellow with jaundice (l. 85).

90   *wilful stillness,* deliberate silence. *entertain,* maintain.

91   *be . . . opinion,* gain the reputation.

92   *conceit,* intelligence, understanding.

GRATIANO: Let me play the fool;
With mirth and laughter let old wrinkles come,   80
And let my liver rather heat with wine
Than my heart cool with mortifying groans.
Why should a man whose blood is warm within,
Sit like his grandsire cut in alabaster?
Sleep when he wakes? and creep into the jaundice
By being peevish? I tell thee what Antonio—
I love thee, and it is my love that speaks—
There are a sort of men whose visages
Do cream and mantle like a standing pond,
And do a wilful stillness entertain,   90
With purpose to be dressed in an opinion
Of wisdom, gravity, profound conceit,

93   *Sir Oracle.* A scornful term for one who thinks his words are so
      important that everyone should listen to them.

94   *let ... bark.* Should Gratiano give a mocking representation by
      voice and gesture?

96–7 *That ... nothing. Proverbs,* xvii. 28. 'Even a fool, when he holdeth
      his peace, is counted wise.'

98–9 *If ... fools,* if they spoke would utter such nonsense that their
      hearers would call them fools and so run into the danger of
      damnation which threatens those who call their brothers fools.
      St. Matthew, v. 22, 'whosoever shall say [to his brother] Thou
      fool! shall be in danger of hell fire.'

100   Is Lorenzo trying to draw Gratiano away or to interrrupt him
      here?

102   *gudgeon,* a small fish. A foolish person ready to believe anything.

104   *I'll ... dinner.* A quick jest at a habit of Puritan preachers.
      exhortation, sermon.
         Possibly Gratiano's description may be a topical hit at a Puritan
      preacher.

106–7 How does Lorenzo say this—bitterly, dully, laughingly, sadly?

108   *moe,* more.

110   *for this gear,* for this business, in view of what you say.

112   *neat's tongue,* ox-tongue.
      maid ... vendible, old maid.
         The jingle adds emphasis to Gratiano's parting witticism. In
      what style do Gratiano and Lorenzo depart—gay, happy-go-
      lucky, confident, assured, swaggering, laughing, sad, pensive?

114– What dramatic purpose does the use of prose serve at this point?
   18 Does this correctly sum up Gratiano's volubility?

115   *reasons,* basic facts.

119   *same,* one.

123   *disabled ... estate,* reduced my wealth.

124   *something,* to some extent. *swelling port,* grander style of living.

125   *faint,* slender, small.

As who should say, 'I am Sir Oracle,
And when I ope my lips let no dog bark'.
O my Antonio, I do not know of these
That therefore only are reputed wise
For saying nothing; when I am very sure
If they should speak, would almost damn those ears
Which hearing them would call their brothers fools.
I'll tell thee more of this another time. 100
But fish not with this melancholy bait
For this fool gudgeon, this opinion.
Come good Lorenzo. Fare ye well awhile,
I'll end my exhortation after dinner.

ORENZO: Well, we will leave you then till dinner-time.
I must be one of these same dumb wise men,
For Gratiano never lets me speak.

GRATIANO: Well, keep me company but two years moe,
Thou shalt not know the sound of thine own tongue.

ANTONIO: Fare you well: I'll grow a talker for this gear. 110

GRATIANO: Thanks i'faith, for silence is only commendable
In a neat's tongue dried, and a maid not vendible.

[*Exeunt Gratiano and Lorenzo*

ANTONIO: Is that any thing now?

BASSANIO: Gratiano speaks an infinite deal of nothing, more than any man in all Venice. His reasons are as two grains of wheat hid in two bushels of chaff: you shall seek all day ere you find them, and when you have them, they are not worth the search.

ANTONIO: Well, tell me now what lady is the same
To whom you swore a secret pilgrimage, 120
That you today promised to tell me of?

BASSANIO: 'Tis not unknown to you Antonio,
How much I have disabled mine estate,
By something showing a more swelling port
Than my faint means would grant continuance;

126 *make . . . abridged,* complain at having to cut down my high standards of living.

128 *fairly,* honourably, or, completely.

129 *time,* time-of-life, youth.

130 *gaged,* pledged.

132–3 *And . . . purposes,* and your love for me justified my declaring to you all my plans and proposals.

136–7 *if . . . honour,* if it may be regarded as honourable just as you yourself are always honourable.

138 *extremest means,* utmost wealth.

139 *occasions,* needs.
   Apparently a not unusual practice.

141 *his . . . flight,* a similar arrow with its feather cut to the seam pattern.

142 *advised,* careful.

143 *forth,* out.

144 *proof,* experience, practice.

144–5 *I . . . innocence,* I stress this . . . because what follows is similarly completely free from deceit.

148 *self,* same.

150 *or,* either.

151 *hazard,* stake, money risked.

153–4 *spend . . . circumstance,* waste time in approaching my love with such round-about arguments.

156 *making . . . uttermost,* doubting that I would do my utmost.

Nor do I now make moan to be abridged
From such a noble rate, but my chief care
Is to come fairly off from the great debts
Wherein my time, something too prodigal,
Hath left me gaged. To you Antonio   130
I owe the most in money and in love,
And from your love I have a warranty
To unburden all my plots and purposes
How to get clear of all the debts I owe.

ANTONIO: I pray you good Bassanio let me know it,
And if it stand as you yourself still do,
Within the eye of honour, be assured
My purse, my person, my extremest means
Lie all unlocked to your occasions.

BASSANIO: In my school days, when I had lost one shaft,   140
I shot his fellow of the self same flight
The self same way, with more advised watch
To find the other forth, and by adventuring both
I oft found both. I urge this childhood proof
Because what follows is pure innocence.
I owe you much, and like a wilful youth,
That which I owe is lost, but if you please
To shoot another arrow that self way
Which you did shoot the first, I do not doubt,
As I will watch the aim, or to find both,   150
Or bring your latter hazard back again,
And thankfully rest debtor for the first.

ANTONIO: You know me well, and herein spend but time
To wind about my love with circumstance;
And out of doubt you do me now more wrong
In making question of my uttermost
Than if you had made waste of all I have.
Then do but say to me what I should do
That in your knowledge may by me be done,

The Merchant of Venice

160   *prest unto*, ready to do.

From what does Bassanio's long delay in answering Antonio's question arise—embarrassment, uncertainty, anxiety to justify himself, wish to soften the blow to Antonio's friendship for him?

161   *richly left*, a wealthy heiress.

162   *fairer . . . word*, better still.

163   *sometimes*, formerly.

163–4   *sometimes . . . messages*. Bassanio interrupts his description with a tender reminiscence.

164   *speechless messages*. Love was thought to begin in the eyes by the exchange of glances.

165   *nothing undervalued*, in no way inferior.

166   *Portia*. The daughter of the Roman Censor, Cato, famous for his attacks on corruption. She was the wife of Brutus, the leader of the conspirators who killed Julius Caesar. Her wisdom, learning, courage, and love for her husband were highly praised.

168   *four winds*, i.e. winds from each 'quarter' of the compass.

170–2   *golden fleece . . . Colchos' strand . . . Jasons*. In Greek legend the hero Jason sailed with his crew the Argonauts, to Colchis in quest of the golden fleece. The fleece was that of the winged ram which carried Phrixas in safety to Colchis. He sacrificed the ram as a thank-offering to Zeus and hung its golden fleece in a grove guarded by a dragon. Jason, aided by the magic of Medea, daughter of the king of Colchis, captured the fleece.

175   *presages . . . thrift*, foretells me of such success.

The three speeches of Bassanio, ll. 122–34, 140–52, 161–76 are constructed in the same way, a preliminary statement followed by a direct address to Antonio. The last one 'O my Antonio', is a climax spoken with intensity and eagerness following the enthusiastic description of Portia. Is his delivery of the last speech in any way different from that of the two preceding ones?

178   *commodity*, merchandise.

It can be assumed that Antonio's wealth was distributed as he tells Salerio and also committed so that he could not recall it.

179   *present sum*, ready money, cash.

181   *racked*, stretched.

182   *furnish . . . Portia*, to equip you suitably for visiting Portia at Belmont.

183   *presently*, immediately.

And I am prest unto it. Therefore speak.   160
BASSANIO: In Belmont is a lady richly left,
And she is fair, and fairer than that word,
Of wondrous virtues—sometimes from her eyes
I did receive fair speechless messages.
Her name is Portia, nothing undervalued
To Cato's daughter, Brutus' Portia.
Nor is the wide world ignorant of her worth,
For the four winds blow in from every coast
Renowned suitors, and her sunny locks
Hang on her temples like a golden fleece,   170
Which makes her seat of Belmont Colchos' strand,
And many Jasons come in quest of her.
O my Antonio, had I but the means
To hold a rival place with one of them,
I have a mind presages me such thrift,
That I should questionless be fortunate.
ANTONIO: Thou know'st that all my fortunes are at sea,
Neither have I money nor commodity
To raise a present sum, therefore go forth;
Try what my credit can in Venice do,   180
That shall be racked even to the uttermost
To furnish thee to Belmont to fair Portia.
Go presently inquire, and so will I,

39

185 *of my trust . . . sake,* on credit or out of friendship.

Which words fit Antonio: generous, charitable, prodigal, ideal friend, ideal Christian, concise in speech, priggish, loving, magnanimous, liberal, patient, intelligent, foolish, righteous, surly?

Many of these widely differing words and phrases have been applied by critics to Bassanio: spendthrift, fortune-hunter, ideal gentleman, aristocratic sponger, poor figure, man of honour; frank, penitent, predatory, prodigal, self-critical, humble, proud, resourceful, tactful, ashamed, embarrassed, in love, romantic, mercenary. Which are applicable?

Belmont

How can the difference between mistress and maid be shown by the way of entry? Do they sit or stand? Do they engage in any occupation—embroidery, needlework, distaff, lute?

Do the opening speeches suggest grandeur, homeliness, hauteur, a fairy-tale castle, simplicity, magnificence, great wealth, affectation or lack of it?

Is it the kind of opening you would expect from Bassanio's praise, I. i, 161–172? Why is prose used?

1 *aweary.* This echo of 'wearies' (I. i, 2) suggests that ll. 1–24 are perhaps a reflection on and a corrective complement to, the previous treatment of Antonio's melancholy.

3–8, Does Nerissa speak severely and reprovingly, brightly or casu-
10 ally?

6 *mean,* small.

7 *seated . . . mean,* occupy a position midway between extremes.
   superfluity, excess, over-indulgence.

7–8 *superfluity . . . longer,* i.e. he who over-indulges himself grows old before his time, but he who has just sufficient for his needs lives the longer.

9 *sentences,* (a) wise sayings, (b) judgements (in law).
   pronounced, (a) spoken, (b) passed (by a judge).

10 *followed,* (a) kept, (b) enforced (in law).

Portia having treated her weariness lightly ('little' . . . 'great') approves with a punning glint of humour Nerissa's advice that happiness is attained by following the 'golden mean'.

12 *chapels.* Originally chapels were small and did not serve parishes.

Where money is, and I no question make
To have it of my trust, or for my sake.   [*Exeunt*

SCENE TWO

Enter PORTIA *and* NERISSA

PORTIA: By my troth Nerissa, my little body is aweary of this
great world.

NERISSA: You would be, sweet madam, if your miseries were
in the same abundance as your good fortunes are; and yet for
aught I see, they are as sick that surfeit with too much, as they
that starve with nothing. It is no mean happiness therefore to
be seated in the mean; superfluity comes sooner by white hairs,
but competency lives longer.

PORTIA: Good sentences, and well pronounced.

NERISSA: They would be better if well followed.   10

PORTIA: If to do were as easy as to to know what were good to
do, chapels had been churches, and poor men's cottages princes'
palaces. It is a good divine that follows his own instructions. I
can easier teach twenty what were good to be done, than be
one of the twenty to follow mine own teaching. The brain may

16   *blood, hot temper,* emotions. It was thought that the varying pro-
      portions of four 'humours', blood, choler, phlegm, and bile, made
      up each person's temperament. Blood was also thought to be the
      source of emotion and passion particularly in youth. A hot
      temper(ament) would have too much choler or blood in its make-
      up.
          Portia's wise sayings (ll. 11–17) seem to be influenced by
      Romans, vii, particularly 18–19 and ii, 20–1.

17   *hare . . . meshes.* Hares were caught by driving them to gaps in a
      hedge in which nets had been spread. The hare was noted for its
      March madness.

18   *reasoning,* discussion.

21   *will,* (*a*) wishes, (*b*) last will.

24, 25 *virtuous, holy, good inspirations.* Nerissa considers that the will
      was divinely inspired and must lead to the right result.

31   *over-name them,* go over their names.

32   *level,* guess.

34   *Neapolitan.* Neapolitan gentlemen were celebrated for their skill
      in horsemanship, then considered an essential part of a gentleman's
      education.

35ff. Portia shows a different reaction to each suitor by pitch of
      voice, expression and perhaps some action or gesture.

35   *colt,* raw young man.

36–7 *makes . . . parts,* considers it an highly apt addition to his other
      accomplishments.

39   *County Palatine.* A vassal lord who, within his own territory, held
      the powers of a king. Here it may refer to a German prince.
          Does Portia mimic his expression or speech?

40   *An,* if.

41   *choose,* please yourself, do the other thing !

42   *weeping philosopher.* The Greek philosopher, Heracleitus of Eph-
      esus, who lived in the 5th and 4th centuries B.C. was so called
      because of his gloomy views on life.

44–5 *death's-head . . . mouth,* speechless skull.

47   *by,* about.
          Le Bon. Is the mention of his name greeted by Portia with
      laughter?

42

devise laws for the blood, but a hot temper leaps o'er a cold decree; such a hare is madness the youth, to skip o'er the meshes of good counsel the cripple. But this reasoning is not in the fashion to choose me a husband. O me, the word 'choose'! I may neither choose whom I would, nor refuse whom I dislike; so is the will of a living daughter curbed by the will of a dead father. Is it not hard Nerissa, that I cannot choose one, nor refuse none? 23

NERISSA: Your father was ever virtuous, and holy men at their death have good inspirations, therefore the lottery that he hath devised in these three chests of gold, silver, and lead, whereof who chooses his meaning chooses you, will no doubt never be chosen by any rightly, but one who shall rightly love. But what warmth is there in your affection towards any of these princely suitors that are already come?

PORTIA: I pray thee over-name them, and as thou namest them, I will describe them, and, according to my description level at my affection. 33

NERISSA: First there is the Neapolitan prince.

PORTIA: Ay that's a colt indeed, for he doth nothing but talk of his horse, and he makes it a great appropriation to his own good parts that he can shoe him himself. I am much afeard my lady his mother played false with a smith.

NERISSA: Then there is the County Palatine.

PORTIA: He doth nothing but frown, as who should say, 'An you will not have me, choose'; he hears merry tales and smiles not; I fear he will prove the weeping philosopher when he grows old, being so full of unmannerly sadness in his youth. I had rather be married to a death's-head with a bone in his mouth than to either of these. God defend me from these two. 46

NERISSA: How say you by the French lord, Monsieur Le Bon?

48   *God . . . man.* he is made in God's image and must therefore be believed to be a man.

        Frenchmen were regarded as excitable, of quick-changing moods, much given to fencing and dancing.

50   *horse better than,* he boasts that his horse is better than the Neapolitan's.

53–4   *twenty husbands,* i.e. since he changes his character so swiftly.

56   *What . . . you,* how do you like?

        say. Emphasize to bring out the quibble.

        Englishmen's inability or refusal to speak foreign languages was notorious even in Shakespeare's time.

60   *court,* law court.

61   *pennyworth,* (*a*) small quantity, (*b*) bargain.

        a . . . picture, a fine figure of a man, a fine appearance.

62   *dumb show,* part of a play acted without speech. Portia may also quibble on 'show' (appearance, spectacle).

63   *suited,* (*a*) dressed, (*b*) dressed to suit himself.

        It was a common joke that Englishmen imitated foreign fashions of dress so clumsily that they appeared in a ludicrous mixture of styles.

        doublet, a jacket fitting tightly from waist to neck.

        round hose, breeches that were well puffed out.

64   *behaviour everywhere.* Another current jibe was 'an Englishman Italianate' is a 'devil incarnate'.

67   *neighbourly charity.* An ironical remark. Possibly an echo of *Romans,* xiii, 7–10.

68   *borrowed . . . of,* received from. This may be an allusion to troubles on the Scottish border in 1596.

69–70   *Frenchman . . . another.* The French frequently pledged themselves to assist the Scots against the English.

70   *sealed under,* signed immediately below the Scot on the document agreeing to repay the Englishman the box on the ear.

74, 76   *best, beast.* A frequent pun. As reasoning power raised man above beasts, drunkenness, by putting this power out of action, reduced a man to a beast.

PORTIA: God made him, and therefore let him pass for a man.
In truth I know it is a sin to be a mocker, but he—why he hath
a horse better than the Neapolitan's, a better bad habit of
frowning than the Count Palatine; he is every man in no man;
if a throstle sing, he falls straight a capering; he will fence with
his own shadow. If I should marry him, I should marry twenty
husbands. If he would despise me, I would forgive him, for if
he love me to madness, I shall never requite him.   55

NERISSA: What say you then to Falconbridge, the young baron
of England?

PORTIA: You know I say nothing to him, for he understands
not me, nor I him; he hath neither Latin, French, nor Italian
and you will come into the court and swear that I have a poor
pennyworth in the English. He is a proper man's picture, but
alas, who can converse with a dumb show? How oddly he is
suited! I think he bought his doublet in Italy, his round hose in
France, his bonnet in Germany, and his behaviour every-
where.   65

NERISSA: What think you of the Scottish lord his neighbour?

PORTIA: That he hath a neighbourly charity in him, for he
borrowed a box of the ear of the Englishman, and swore he
would pay him again when he was able. I think the Frenchman
became his surety and sealed under for another.

NERISSA: How like you the young German, the Duke of
Saxony's nephew?   72

PORTIA: Very vilely in the morning when he is sober, and most
vilely in the afternoon when he is drunk. When he is best, he is
a little worse than a man, and when he is worst, he is little
better than a beast. An the worst fall that ever fell, I hope I shall
make shift to go without him.

NERISSA: If he should offer to choose, and choose the right
casket, you should refuse to perform your father's will, if you
should refuse to accept him.   80

PORTIA: Therefore for fear of the worst, I pray thee set a deep

82   *rhenish,* white wine of the Rhine district.
       contrary, wrong.
          Is Portia serious? What is her mood—reckless, mocking, high
       spirited, vivacious, satirical, desperate, alarmed?
84   *sponge,* drunkard.

88   *sort,* way, manner.
89   *father's imposition,* the conditions imposed by your father.
90   *Sibylla.* In Roman story the sibyl (prophetess) of Cumae offered
       three prophetic books to Tarquin. Apollo promised her that she
       should live for as many years as the grains of sand she was holding
       in her hand.
          Portia, at this point, is grateful for the protection given her by
       the strict conditions of her father's will.
91   *Diana,* the moon or huntress-goddess, protector of maidens.
92   *parcel,* set. It is not used contemptuously by Shakespeare.
93   *dote on,* am deeply in love with.
       absence. Perhaps a slight pause beforehand emphasizes this anti-
       climax.
96   *scholar . . . soldier.* One of the highest compliments that could be
       paid to a gentleman.
       Yes . . . called. Portia remembers with quick eagerness and then
       checks her impulse to avoid betraying her feelings to Nerissa.

104   *four.* There were six. See Introduction p. 5.

110   *condition,* character, temperament.
110-1 *complexion,* i.e. a black face. Devils were believed to have black
       complexions.
          'complexion' originally meant 'temperament', later it was
       applied to the colour and texture of the skin as revealing the
       temperament within. Portia describes an impossibility.

glass of rhenish wine on the contrary casket, for if the devil be within, and that temptation without, I know he will choose it. I will do any thing Nerissa, ere I'll be married to a sponge.

NERISSA: You need not fear lady the having any of these lords. They have acquainted me with their determinations, which is indeed to return to their home, and to trouble you with no more suit, unless you may be won by some other sort than your father's imposition, depending on the caskets.

PORTIA: If I live to be as old as Sibylla, I will die as chaste as Diana, unless I be obtained by the manner of my father's will. I am glad this parcel of wooers are so reasonable, for there is not one among them but I dote on his very absence; and I pray God grant them a fair departure.   94

NERISSA: Do you not remember lady, in your father's time, a Venetian, a scholar and a soldier, that came hither in company of the Marquis of Montferrat?

PORTIA: Yes, yes, it was Bassanio, as I think so was he called.

NERISSA: True madam, he of all the men that ever my foolish eyes looked upon, was the best deserving a fair lady.

PORTIA: I remember him well, and I remember him worthy of thy praise.   102

Enter a Serving-man

How now, what news?

SERVING-MAN: The four strangers seek for you madam to take their leave; and there is a forerunner come from a fifth, the Prince of Morocco, who brings word the prince his master will be here tonight.   107

PORTIA: If I could bid the fifth welcome with so good a heart as I can bid the other four farewell, I should be glad of his approach. If he have the condition of a saint, and the com-

111   *shrive me,* hear my confession (as a saint).

Immediately after mention of Bassanio the announcement of a fifth suitor is probably intended to raise expectations in the audience. That he is the Prince of Morocco is a shock and raises the tension because the Elizabethans believed Moors to be savage, lustful and devilish.

108– Portia's words show that she is disconcerted and serious if not
12   anxious.

113– The jingle of rhyme is perhaps intended to end the scene on a
15   sprightly, mocking note in keeping with the descriptions of the suitors.

What values to the play have the descriptions of the suitors: a string of topical jokes, a proof of Portia's desirability or fame, a justification of the terms of the will in frightening away inadequate suitors, a revealing of Portia's human qualities irked at the will yet gay, spirited, critical in taste and discrimination, witty, loyal, and of great integrity, a sop for the 'groundlings'?

What words fit Nerissa: stolid, vivacious, moralizing, frivolous, practical, priggish, grave, pious, sprightly, wise? Are there any contrasting qualities in her character? If so, what dramatic purposes do they serve? Is she older or younger than Portia? Is she a chaperone, a waiting gentlewoman, a confidant, a chambermaid?

Venice

Who enters first? Why?

Shylock's first appearance is important. Is he dignified, virile, sinister, comic, suspicious, grotesque, arrogant? Is the impression conveyed by bearing, clothing, mannerisms, voice? Is his speaking high-pitched, nasal, staccato, drawling, lisping, rasping, quiet, with some letters slurred, in mephistophelian bass, 'lickerish'?

1–9 Why are certain phrases repeated? Is Shylock thinking them over, or making mental or written notes? The first three words reveal one aspect of his character.

1   *ducats,* Italian gold coins worth then about 4s. 8d.
     well, yes, I have or understand that.

4   *be bound,* offer himself as surety.

6   *may,* can.
     stead, help.

6–7 The three rapid questions show Bassanio's impatience and irritation at Shylock's non-committal replies.

plexion of a devil, I had rather he should shrive me than wive me.

Come Nerissa. Sirrah go before.

Whiles we shut the gates upon one wooer, another knocks at the door.

Exeunt

SCENE THREE

Enter BASSANIO *and* SHYLOCK

SHYLOCK: Three thousand ducats—well.

BASSANIO: Ay sir, for three months.

SHYLOCK: For three months—well.

BASSANIO: For the which as I told you, Antonio shall be bound.

SHYLOCK: Antonio shall become bound—well.

BASSANIO: May you stead me? Will you pleasure me? Shall I know your answer?

11   *good*, sound financially. Shylock may, however, be sneering at Antonio's 'goodness', but quickly explains the word in the commercial sense when Bassanio shows indignation.

14   *sufficient*, acceptable as a surety.
15   *in supposition*, uncertain.

17   *Rialto*. The exchange in Venice where merchants carried out their business.
18   *squandered*, foolishly and recklessly scattered abroad.
20   *pirates*. The danger from Barbary pirates, particularly in the Mediterranean Sea, was considerable.

24   *Be assured*, have no doubts.
25   *be assured*, obtain guarantees.

28-32 *Yes ... you*. This may be spoken aside while Bassanio turns towards Antonio.
28-9 *habitation ... into*, i.e. pork. The miraculous healing by Jesus of the man possessed with devils. The devils on leaving the man entered into a herd of swine which rushed into the sea. (*St. Matthew*, viii).
29   *Nazarite*, Nazarene.
      The purely business preliminaries have been in prose. As the merchant of Venice and the Jew face each other, the quickening interest and deepening emotion are emphasized by verse rhythms.

35   *fawning publican*. The publicans mentioned in the Gospels were the hated Jewish 'collaborators' who collected taxes from their countrymen for the Romans.
      fawning. Many explanations have been offered.
      (*a*) The downcast Antonio is affectionately greeting Bassanio who is apparently of higher rank (Lord Bassanio?) i.e. he is a servant

SHYLOCK: Three thousand ducats for three months, and Antonio bound.

BASSANIO: Your answer to that.   10

SHYLOCK: Antonio is a good man.

BASSANIO: Have you heard any imputation to the contrary?

SHYLOCK: Ho no, no, no, no. My meaning in saying he is a good man, is to have you understand me that he is sufficient— yet his means are in supposition: he hath an argosy bound to Tripolis, another to the Indies; I understand moreover upon the Rialto, he hath a third at Mexico, a fourth for England, and other ventures he hath squandered abroad. But ships are but boards, sailors but men; there be land-rats and water-rats, water-thieves and land-thieves, I mean pirates, and then there is the peril of waters, winds, and rocks. The man is notwithstanding sufficient. Three thousand ducats—I think I may take his bond.   23

BASSANIO: Be assured you may.

SHYLOCK: I will be assured I may. And that I may be assured, I will bethink me. May I speak with Antonio?

BASSANIO: If it please you to dine with us.

SHYLOCK: Yes, to smell pork, to eat of the habitation which your prophet the Nazarite conjured the devil into. I will buy with you, sell with you, talk with you, walk with you, and so following. But I will not eat with you, drink with you, nor pray with you. What news on the Rialto? Who is he comes here?   33

Enter ANTONIO

BASSANIO: This is Signior Antonio.

SHYLOCK: [*Aside*] How like a fawning publican he looks.

of the Gentile oppressors who robbed the Jews of their lawful gains (Arden).

(b) It refers to the parable of the scornful Pharisee and the humble publican (*St. Luke*, xviii. 10–14).

(c) Antonio is a currish publican in that he is about to ask a Jew, Shylock, for money.

In any case the phrase is two-edged. To Shylock the publican was a currish outcast; the audience, however, might remember the humble publican who was justified above the Pharisee (Shylock), and that Jesus was the friend of publicans.

36   *I hate . . . Christian.* Like the Vice in the morality plays, Shylock declares in an aside his hatred of goodness.

37   *in low simplicity,* (a) in the depth of folly, (b) humble sincerity.

39   *usance,* usury, interest on loans of money.

40   *upon the hip,* at a disadvantage. In wrestling one of the positions leading to a throw. It may refer to the angel who wrestled with Jacob and injured his hip. (*Genesis,* xxxii).

41   *ancient grudge,* i.e. as between Jew and Christian.

44   *thrift,* profit. To call usury 'thrift' was proper in Shylock's eyes since it was the Christian religion, not the Jewish, that had forbidden the charging of interest.

Shylock has announced his hatred, his motives, religious, racial and commercial and his vengeful intentions in confidence to the audience. He now sets out to trap Antonio.

46   *Shylock . . . hear?* Any stage business?

49   *gross,* total sum.

53   *Rest . . . fair.* Is Antonio reluctant to approach Shylock or does Shylock pretend not to see him?

53–4   *Rest . . . mouths.* A mocking piece of irony and hypocrisy.

55–8   *Shylock . . . custom.* This sacrifice of his principles out of friendship disturbs Antonio deeply. He speaks abruptly and with effort.

56   *taking . . . giving . . . excess,* receiving interest from lending money nor paying interest on borrowed money.
       excess, interest.

57   *ripe,* immediate, that have come to a head.

58   *possessed,* informed.

Shylock tries to entice Antonio to give up his high principled opposition to usury. This speech attempts to find scriptural support for usury, and in so doing suggests that Shylock's character is pious and upright. It involves Antonio in a discussion and the delay makes him more impatient.

I hate him for he is a Christian.
But more, for that in low simplicity
He lends out money gratis, and brings down
The rate of usance here with us in Venice.
If I can catch him once upon the hip,   40
I will feed fat the ancient grudge I bear him.
He hates our sacred nation, and he rails
Even there where merchants most do congregate,
On me, my bargains, and my well-won thrift,
Which he calls interest. Cursed be my tribe
If I forgive him.
BASSANIO: Shylock, do you hear?
SHYLOCK: I am debating of my present store,
And by the near guess of my memory
I cannot instantly raise up the gross
Of full three thousand ducats. What of that?   50
Tubal a wealthy Hebrew of my tribe,
Will furnish me. But soft, how many months
Do you desire? [*To Antonio*] Rest you fair good signior,
Your worship was the last man in our mouths.
ANTONIO: Shylock, although I neither lend nor borrow
By taking nor by giving of excess,
Yet to supply the ripe wants of my friend,
I'll break a custom. Is he yet possessed
How much ye would?
SHYLOCK: Ay, ay, three thousand ducats.
ANTONIO: And for three months.   60
SHYLOCK: I had forgot—three months, you told me so.
Well then, your bond; and let me see—but hear you,

64   *upon advantage*, at interest.

65   *Jacob . . . sheep. Genesis*, xxx, 31–43.

67   *As . . . behalf. Genesis*, xxvii, 6–45.

72   *compromised*, agreed.
73   *eanlings*, new-born lambs.
74   *hire*, wages.

78   *pilled*, peeled, stripped.

80   *fulsome*, fat.
81   *eaning time*, lambing time.
82   *Fall*, give birth to.
83   *thrive*, (a) prosper, (b) gain interest (profit).
84   *thrift*, interest.
      Jacob made profit (interest) by his skill in sheep-breeding and
      was so blessed by God. In the same way interest (profit) is blessed
      as long as it has not been obtained by theft.
85   *served for*, i.e. these were Jacob's wages as a servant. If Antonio
      accepts this argument, well-known to be false, he denies his
      principles and could be called a turn-coat for the sake of money.
      He scornfully rejects it implying (l. 92) that Shylock is tempting
      him.
87   *But . . . heaven.* Possibly a reference to *Genesis*, xxxi, 7–13.
88   *inserted*, in Scripture or into the conversation.
89   *Or . . . rams.* It was held to be contrary to Nature for money to
      breed, i.e. metal was barren (l. 128).
91–6 *Mark . . . hath.* Antonio draws Bassanio aside.
92   *The . . . purpose. St. Matthew*, iv, 6; *St. Luke*, iv, 10.

Methought you said, you neither lend nor borrow
Upon advantage.
ANTONIO: I do never use it.
SHYLOCK: When Jacob grazed his uncle Laban's sheep—
This Jacob from our holy Abram was,
As his wise mother wrought in his behalf,
The third possessor; ay, he was the third—
ANTONIO: And what of him? did he take interest?
SHYLOCK: No, not take interest, not as you would say 70
Directly interest; mark what Jacob did.
When Laban and himself were compromised
That all the eanlings which were streaked and pied
Should fall as Jacob's hire, the ewes being rank
In end of autumn turned to the rams,
And when the work of generation was
Between these woolly breeders in the act,
The skilful shepherd pilled me certain wands
And in the doing of the deed of kind
He stuck them up before the fulsome ewes, 80
Who then conceiving, did in eaning time
Fall parti-coloured lambs, and those were Jacob's.
This was a way to thrive, and he was blest;
And thrift is blessing if men steal it not.
ANTONIO: This was a venture sir, that Jacob served for,
A thing not in his power to bring to pass,
But swayed and fashioned by the hand of heaven.
Was this inserted to make interest good?
Or is your gold and silver ewes and rams?
SHYLOCK: I cannot tell, I make it breed as fast. 90
But note me signior.
ANTONIO: Mark you this Bassanio,
The devil can cite Scripture for his purpose.
An evil soul producing holy witness
Is like a villain with a smiling cheek,

97 *Three ... sum.* Is this spoken aside, triumphantly, 'lickerishly', or thoughtfully?

99 *beholding,* indebted, under obligation.

100ff. *Signior ...* Any change in Shylock's manner and delivery?

   Shylock having involved Antonio in a discussion now links their personal relationship to the loan. He shifts his ground thinking ahead of his offer to come and ironically twists the argument: because I lent money, you have abused me; because you abused me, shall I lend you money?

101 *rated,* reviled, spoken angrily to.

102 *usances,* usury.

103 *Still,* always.

104 *sufferance,* suffering, patience.

   badge, mark. Perhaps suggested by the yellow cap worn as a distinguishing mark by the Venetian Jews.

106 *gaberdine,* long cloak. There may have been a standard form of dress for Jews in the Elizabethan theatre (Reynolds *Staging of Elizabethan Plays*).

107 *And ... own.* St. Matthew, xx, 15 (IV. i, 98).

   use, (a) making use of, (b) gainful use (of money).

111 *did ... rheum,* did spit.

113 *suit,* request.

   The marked variations in rhythm reflect Shylock's feelings. Is he calculating, resentful, sarcastic, malevolent, indignant, justified, proud, ironic, wronged, laughing up his sleeve?

   By what movements and gestures do Antonio and Bassanio shew their reactions during this speech?

127–8 Possibly an echo of *Deuteronomy*, xxiii, 19–20.

128 *breed,* interest. 'breed' and 'barren' are deliberately opposed.

A goodly apple rotten at the heart.
O what a goodly outside falsehood hath.
SHYLOCK: Three thousand ducats—'tis a good round sum.
   Three months from twelve—then let me see, the rate—
ANTONIO: Well Shylock, shall we be beholding to you?
SHYLOCK: Signior Antonio, many a time and oft   100
   In the Rialto you have rated me
   About my moneys and my usances.
   Still have I borne it with a patient shrug,
   For sufferance is the badge of all our tribe.
   You call me misbeliever, cut-throat dog,
   And spit upon my Jewish gaberdine,
   And all for use of that which is mine own.
   Well then, it now appears you need my help.
   Go to then, you come to me, and you say,
   'Shylock, we would have moneys'—you say so;   110
   You that did void your rheum upon my beard,
   And foot me as you spurn a stranger cur
   Over your threshold—moneys is your suit.
   What should I say to you? Should I not say,
   'Hath a dog money? Is it possible
   A cur can lend three thousand ducats?' Or
   Shall I bend low, and in a bondman's key
   With bated breath, and whispering humbleness
   Say this:
   'Fair sir, you spit on me on Wednesday last,   120
   You spurned me such a day, another time
   You called me dog; and for these courtesies
   I'll lend you thus much moneys'?
ANTONIO: I am as like to call thee so again,
   To spit on thee again, to spurn thee too.
   If thou wilt lend this money, lend it not
   As to thy friends, for when did friendship take
   A breed for barren metal of his friend?

130   *break,* fail to pay on the day appointed.

        Shylock's speech implies that Antonio should have behaved in a friendlier fashion if he wants money. Antonio, his pride stung by Shylock's ironic, patronizing air, and the half invitation to retract his attitude, refuses to surrender his principles or to change his behaviour. The latter might well have made him appear a 'fawning publican' who changed his tune for money.

        Antonio shouts that usury between friends is unthinkable, as far as Shylock is concerned with his practice of usury he can treat Antonio as his enemy. It is a natural but fatal reply for Shylock's speech had led to it; it is a striking piece of dramatic irony (for Shylock has declared himself Antonio's enemy) and a reckless challenge to fate. It gives Shylock his cue. Picking up Antonio's distinction between friendship and enmity, with bland deceit he offers friendship and an interest-free loan. Antonio's arguments are undermined, and he accepts the offer.

133   *stained,* disgraced.

134   *doit,* a very small Dutch coin, jot.

136   *kind,* (*a*) generous, (*b*) natural.

137   *notary,* solicitor.

138   *single bond,* i.e. with no conditions attached.

138,   *merry* . . . , *merry* . . . Shylock's cheerful good fellowship leads
166   Antonio from his melancholy and anger into rash confidence.

142   *nominated for,* named as.
        equal, exact.

147–8   Is the rhyme accidental or has it a purpose?

153–5   *O* . . . *others.* Hypocritical pious horror and dramatic irony.

But lend it rather to thine enemy,
Who if he break, thou mayst with better face   130
Exact the penalty.
SHYLOCK: Why look you how you storm.
I would be friends with you, and have your love,
Forget the shames that you have stained me with,
Supply your present wants, and take no doit
Of usance for my moneys—and you'll not hear me.
This is kind I offer.
BASSANIO: This were kindness.
SHYLOCK: This kindness will I show—
Go with me to a notary, seal me there
Your single bond, and in a merry sport,
If you repay me not on such a day,
In such a place, such sum or sums as are   140
Expressed in the condition, let the forfeit
Be nominated for an equal pound
Of your fair flesh, to be cut off and taken
In what part of your body pleaseth me.
ANTONIO: Content, i'faith, I'll seal to such a bond,
And say there is much kindness in the Jew.
BASSANIO: You shall not seal to such a bond for me,
I'll rather dwell in my necessity.
ANTONIO: Why fear not man, I will not forfeit it.
Within these two months, that's a month before   150
This bond expires, I do expect return
Of thrice three times the value of this bond.
SHYLOCK: O father Abram, what these Christians are,
Whose own hard dealings teaches them suspect
The thoughts of others. Pray you tell me this,
If he should break his day, what should I gain
By the exaction of the forfeiture?
A pound of man's flesh taken from a man
Is not so estimable, profitable neither,

163   *for . . . love,* for the sake of my love.

168   *fearful,* unreliable, timid.
169   *unthrifty,* careless, wasteful ('unprofitable'), (Compare II. v, 45–7).
       presently, immediately.

170   *Hie,* haste.

172   *terms,* words, or the 'terms' of the bond.

As flesh of muttons, beefs, or goats. I say, 160
To buy his favour, I extend this friendship.
If he will take it, so, if not, adieu,
And for my love I pray you wrong me not.

ANTONIO: Yes Shylock, I will seal unto this bond.

SHYLOCK: Then meet me forthwith at the notary's.
Give him direction for this merry bond,
And I will go and purse the ducats straight,
See to my house, left in the fearful guard
Of an unthrifty knave; and presently
I will be with you.

ANTONIO: Hie thee gentle Jew.   [*Exit Shylock*
The Hebrew will turn Christian, he grows kind. 171

BASSANIO: I like not fair terms, and a villain's mind.

ANTONIO: Come on, in this there can be no dismay,
My ships come home a month before the day.   [*Exeunt*

'Flourish Cornets' The brisk burst of music following suddenly the disputes of the last scene challenges the attention of the audience to a contrasting scene of dignity and rich pageantry.

To bring out the allegorical aspect of Morocco as the life of the senses, the scene should be played in the style of tapestry almost a tableaux.

It is helpful to assume that the rest of the play is not known. Then this first serious attempt to win Portia increases the tension and suspense Bassanio may yet arrive too late. Will chance alone decide whom Portia marries? By what means will the correct choice be made?

The entries should be made from opposite doors.

Does Portia sit?

With what movements do they greet each other?

1   *complexion*. Four syllables.

2   *shadowed livery*, shaded badge.
      burnished, glowing.

5   *Phoebus*, the sun.

6   *make incision*, cut our flesh.

6–7   *make . . . mine*, Morocco implies that whatever the colour of their skins there is no difference in the colour of their blood.

      There may be a reference to boastful young gallants who sometimes stabbed themselves in the arm and drank a health to their lady in blood.

8   *aspect*, face.

9   *feared*, frightened.

12   *steal . . . thoughts*, gain your affections.

13   *terms*, matters.

13–14   *I . . . eyes*. A gentle rebuke.

14   *nice direction*, fastidious guidance.

17   *scanted*, limited.

18   *wit*, (a) wisdom, (b) testament, will (Hulme).

20   *fair*. A glance at Morocco's complexion.

25   *Sophy*, the Shah of Persia.

ACT TWO

SCENE ONE

Flourish Cornets. Enter the PRINCE OF MOROCCO (*a tawny Moor all in white*) *and three or four followers accordingly; with* PORTIA, NERISSA, *and their train*

MOROCCO: Mislike me not for my complexion,
  The shadowed livery of the burnished sun,
  To whom I am a neighbour, and near bred.
  Bring me the fairest creature northward born,
  Where Phœbus' fire scarce thaws the icicles,
  And let us make incision for your love,
  To prove whose blood is reddest, his or mine.
  I tell thee lady, this aspect of mine
  Hath feared the valiant. By my love I swear
  The best-regarded virgins of our clime   10
  Have loved it too. I would not change this hue,
  Except to steal your thoughts, my gentle queen.
PORTIA: In terms of choice I am not solely led
  By nice direction of a maiden's eyes;
  Besides, the lottery of my destiny
  Bars me the right of voluntary choosing.
  But if my father had not scanted me,
  And hedged me by his wit to yield myself
  His wife who wins me by that means I told you,
  Yourself, renowned prince, then stood as fair   20
  As any comer I have looked on yet
  For my affection.
MOROCCO: Even for that I thank you.
  Therefore I pray you lead me to the caskets
  To try my fortune. By this scimitar
  That slew the Sophy, and a Persian prince

26   *Sultan Solyman,* Suleiman, the Magnificent, Sultan of Turkey, 1490–1566, who was constantly at war with the Persians.

32   *Hercules.* In classical story the semi-divine hero who performed feats of great strength and courage, in particular the 'twelve labours'.

       Lichas. The young servant who brought Hercules the shirt poisoned in the blood of Nessus, the centaur. Hercules in his death-agony threw Lichas into the sea.

35   *Alcides,* Hercules, so called because he was the grandson of Alceus.

       rage, rashness (i.e. in undertaking the game) (Hulme); 'page' has also been suggested.

36   *And . . . I.* Morocco implies that he is to be compared with Hercules.

       blind Fortune. The goddess Fortune who was depicted blindfold on a wheel because of the uncertainty with which good or bad fortune befell men.

       Morocco is concerned with outward appearance and sensual life. He swears that he will accomplish prodigious feats of valour to win Portia in order to create an impression of courage. He assumes that success in making the right choice depends wholly on an outside agency, luck or Fortune, and not on the chooser's character.

42   *be advised,* consider carefully.

43   *Nor . . . not,* nor, indeed, will I speak to a lady afterwards.

44   *to . . . temple,* i.e. to take the oath to abide by the conditions of the choice.

45   *hazard,* risk, chance.

46   *blest,* blessedest.

       Which of the following words are applicable to Morocco: proud, boastful, stupid, unintelligent, magnificent, posturing, simple, frank, fierce, warlike, swaggering, bombastic, superficial?

That won three fields of Sultan Solyman,
I would o'erstare the sternest eyes that look,
Outbrave the heart most daring on the earth,
Pluck the young sucking cubs from the she-bear,
Yea, mock the lion when he roars for prey,   30
To win thee lady. But, alas the while,
If Hercules and Lichas play at dice
Which is the better man, the greater throw
May turn by fortune from the weaker hand:
So is Alcides beaten by his rage,
And so may I, blind Fortune leading me,
Miss that which one unworthier may attain,
And die with grieving.

PORTIA: You must take your chance,
And either not attempt to choose at all,
Or swear before you choose, if you choose wrong   40
Never to speak to lady afterward
In way of marriage, therefore be advised.

MOROCCO: Nor will not. Come bring me unto my chance.

PORTIA: First forward to the temple, after dinner
Your hazard shall be made.

MOROCCO: Good fortune then,
To make me blest or cursed'st among men.

                                        [*Cornets. Exeunt*

65

Venice

It was well-known that the Clown in Elizabethan drama was descended
from the Vice of the Morality plays, and allusions to his Vice-like nature
are common. The point of this soliloquy is that Launcelot, recognizable
as a Clown from his dress, appears absurdly in the unexpected character
of the victim of the Vice, the tempted not the tempter, anxious about his
conscience—the last thing a Vice or Clown possessed.

His dress would be russet jerkin and breeches, boots and a buttoned cap.

How should he enter: acrobatically, swaggeringly, stealthily, pensively,
at a run, in a fluster, in melancholy mood?

1	*will serve,* will have to permit.
2–3	*the fiend . . . me.* Dialogues between conscience and a Vice or the Devil were common in morality plays. Conscience, or the good angel traditionally is on Gobbo's left hand, the fiend on his right.
3ff.	*Gobbo . . .* Should Launcelot mimic the voices of the fiend and his conscience?
6–7	*as aforesaid.* A legal phrase coming oddly from Launcelot.
7–8	*scorn . . . heels.* A quibble. 'to scorn with heels'—to despise utterly.
8	*courageous,* (*a*) brave, (*b*) fierce, wrathful.
	pack, be off.
9	*Fia,* via, forward! Dover Wilson suggests a play on 'fia' and 'fi-end'.
	away . . . fiend. Is this a translation of 'Fia' given 'aside' to the audience?
	for . . . heavens, by Heaven! An odd expression for a devil.
10	*rouse . . . run.* An unusual way of showing courage.
11	*conscience . . . heart,* his conscience hindering what his heart desires like a timid wife clinging to her husband's neck.
14	*something,* somewhat. *smack,* have a taste for. *grow to,* lean towards.
19, 21	*God . . . mark, saving . . . reverence.* Apologetic phrases to preserve the speaker from evil following mention of the Devil. The second may be addressed to his conscience.
22	*incarnation,* incarnate. 'incarnation' = red.

Is this soliloquy a kind of comic contradiction in which the
fiend advises him to escape from hell, purely to amuse the audience?
Has it a more serious significance, a hint of something underlying
an escape from Shylock?

Is it a kind of comic echo of Antonio's situation?

What kind of stage business would be appropriate here?

SCENE TWO

Enter LAUNCELOT

LAUNCELOT: Certainly my conscience will serve me to run
from this Jew my master. The fiend is at mine elbow, and
tempts me, saying to me, 'Gobbo, Launcelot Gobbo, good
Launcelot', or 'good Gobbo', or 'good Launcelot Gobbo, use
your legs, take the start, run away'. My conscience says, 'No,
take heed honest Launcelot, take heed honest Gobbo', or as
aforesaid, 'honest Launcelot Gobbo; do not run, scorn running
with thy heels'. Well, the most courageous fiend bids me pack:
'Fia!' says the fiend; 'away!' says the fiend; 'for the heavens,
rouse up a brave mind', says the fiend, 'and run.' Well, my
conscience, hanging about the neck of my heart, says very
wisely to me: 'My honest friend Launcelot, being an honest
man's son', or rather an honest woman's son—for indeed my
father did something smack, something grow to, he had a
kind of taste—well, my conscience says, 'Launcelot budge
not'. 'Budge', says the fiend. 'Budge not', says my conscience.
'Conscience', say I, 'you counsel well.' 'Fiend', say I, 'you
counsel well.' To be ruled by my conscience, I should stay
with the Jew my master, who—God bless the mark—is a kind
of devil; and to run away from the Jew I should be ruled by
the fiend, who—saving your reverence—is the devil himself.
Certainly the Jew is the very devil incarnation, and in my
conscience, my conscience is but a kind of hard conscience, to
offer to counsel me to stay with the Jew. The fiend gives the
more friendly counsel. I will run, fiend; my heels are at your
command, I will run.   26

30   *sand-blind*, half-blind, with a quibble on the usual meaning of 'sand'.

      gravel-blind, i.e. more than 'sand-blind' but not 'stone-blind'.

31   *confusions*. Launcelot may glance at 'try conclusions', but 'confusions' aptly describes what follows. His 'confusions' are for the most part contradictions or inversions, if fiend is friendly, show courage by running away, etc.

38   *God's sonties*, God's saints.

41   *Master*. A title of respect.

42   *waters*, tears.

46   *well to live*, well off. Gobbo probably thought it meant 'in good health'.

49   *Your . . . sir*, he is your worship's friend, but plain Launcelot.

53   *ergo*, therefore. A word used in logic frequently used with mock learning by clowns. It is a part of Launcelot's 'confusions' that his father addresses him as master in inquiring about Launcelot to whom he refuses to give the title 'Master'.

55   *Fates and Destinies, Sisters Three*. The three goddesses of classical myth, Clotho, Lachesis and Atropos, who wove the pattern of every human life, ending it by cutting off the completed pattern. 'Destinies' may, however, refer to some superstitious practice of telling the future forbidden by the Church (see quotation by Owst, *Literature and Pulpit*, p. 112).

      sayings, maxims.

56, 57   *deceased, gone to heaven*. Which does 'plain terms' suit?

58   *God forbid*. What should be forbidden?

68

Act Two, Scene Two

Enter OLD GOBBO *with a basket*

GOBBO: Master young man, you I pray you, which is the way to master Jew's?

LAUNCELOT: [*Aside*] O heavens, this is my true-begotten father, who being more than sand-blind, high-gravel blind, knows me not—I will try confusions with him.

GOBBO: Master young gentleman, I pray you which is the way to master Jew's?

LAUNCELOT: Turn up on your right hand at the next turning, but at the next turning of all on your left; marry at the very next turning turn of no hand, but turn down indirectly to the Jew's house.   37

GOBBO: By God's sonties 'twill be a hard way to hit. Can you tell me whether one Launcelot that dwells with him, dwell with him or no?

LAUNCELOT: Talk you of young Master Launcelot? [*Aside*] Mark me now, now will I raise the waters. Talk you of young Master Launcelot?

GOBBO: No master sir, but a poor man's son. His father, though I say it, is an honest exceeding poor man, and God be thanked, well to live.   46

LAUNCELOT: Well, let his father be what 'a will, we talk of young Master Launcelot.

GOBBO: Your worship's friend and Launcelot sir.

LAUNCELOT: But I pray you, ergo old man, ergo I beseech you, talk you of young Master Launcelot.

GOBBO: Of Launcelot an't please your mastership.   52

LAUNCELOT: Ergo Master Launcelot. Talk not of Master Launcelot father; for the young gentleman—according to Fates and Destinies and such odd sayings, the Sisters Three and such branches of learning—is indeed deceased, or, as you would say in plain terms, gone to heaven.

GOBBO: Marry God forbid, the boy was the very staff of my age, my very prop.

68   *it . . . child*. The proverb is aptly turned round.

70   *truth . . . hid*. Two more proverbs delivered with emphasis.

75–6   *I . . . shall be*. What gestures and delivery would be appropriate to this anti-climax?

82–3   *Lord . . . be*, O Lord (may He be worshipped).
83   *beard*. The traditional stage business is that Launcelot should kneel with his back to his father.
84   *fill-horse*, cart-horse. 'fill', a shaft.

86–7   *backward*, shorter, i.e. Launcelot has no hair on his face.

92–3   *set . . . rest*, (a) determined, staked my all on, (b) set up house. Further 'confusions' on 'rest . . . run away' and 'not rest . . . run some ground'.

LAUNCELOT: Do I look like a cudgel, or a hovel-post, a staff, or a prop? Do you know me father?   61

GOBBO: Alack the day, I know you not young gentleman, but I pray you tell me, is my boy—God rest his soul—alive or dead?

LAUNCELOT: Do you not know me father?

GOBBO: Alack sir I am sand-blind, I know you not.

LAUNCELOT: Nay indeed, if you had your eyes, you might fail of the knowing me: it is a wise father that knows his own child. Well, old man, I will tell you news of your son—give me your blessing—truth will come to light. Murder cannot be hid long, a man's son may, but at the length truth will out.   71

GOBBO: Pray you sir stand up, I am sure you are not Launcelot, my boy.

LAUNCELOT: Pray you, let's have no more fooling about it, but give me your blessing. I am Launcelot your boy that was, your son that is, your child that shall be.

GOBBO: I cannot think you are my son.

LAUNCELOT: I know not what I shall think of that; but I am Launcelot the Jew's man, and I am sure Margery your wife is my mother.   80

GOBBO: Her name is Margery indeed. I'll be sworn if thou be Launcelot, thou art mine own flesh and blood. Lord worshipped might he be, what a beard hast thou got; thou hast got more hair on thy chin than Dobbin my fill-horse has on his tail.

LAUNCELOT: It should seem then that Dobbin's tail grows backward. I am sure he had more hair of this tail than I have of my face when I last saw him.

GOBBO: Lord how art thou changed. How dost thou and thy master agree? I have brought him a present. How 'gree you now?   91

LAUNCELOT: Well, well, but for mine own part, as I have set up my rest to run away, so I will not rest till I have run some

94   *very*, utter.

95   *tell*, count.

96   *finger . . . ribs*. Launcelot interchanges 'ribs' and 'finger'. Any stage business?

98   *liveries*, servants' uniforms bearing the coat-of-arms of their master.

102   *five of the clock*. Supper was usually taken about 5.30 to 6 p.m. The traditional stage business is for Launcelot to push his father forward, then to bob in front as he interrupts him, and then to retreat behind him again.

108,   *poor, poor*, unfortunate, needy.
  109

111   *infection*, i.e. affection, liking, desire.

116   *scarce*, (*a*) scarcely, (*b*) stingy (Arden).
      cater cousins, close friends.

119   *frutify*. Usually explained as a confusion of 'notify' and 'fructify'. Launcelot may mean, however, that his father will declare the fruits (results) of Shylock's wrong doing. There may be a glance too at the *un*likelihood of an old man having children.

120–1 *I . . . worship*. Does 'frutify unto' suggest to Old Gobbo that it is time he should present his offering to Bassanio?

122   *impertinent*, i.e. pertinent.

ground. My master's a very Jew. Give him a present? give
him a halter. I am famished in his service; you may tell every
finger I have with my ribs. Father I am glad you are come,
give me your present to one Master Bassanio, who indeed
gives rare new liveries. If I serve not him, I will run as far as
God has any ground. O rare fortune, here comes the man. To
him father, for I am a Jew if I serve the Jew any longer.   100

Enter BASSANIO *with* LEONARDO *and a follower or two*

BASSANIO: You may do so, but let it be so hasted that supper
  be ready at the farthest by five of the clock. See these letters
  delivered, put the liveries to making, and desire Gratiano to
  come anon to my lodging.   [*Exit a Servant*
LAUNCELOT: To him father.
GOBBO: God bless your worship.
BASSANIO: Gramercy, wouldst thou aught with me?
GOBBO: Here's my son sir, a poor boy
LAUNCELOT: Not a poor boy sir, but the rich Jew's man that
  would sir—as my father shall specify—   110
GOBBO: He hath a great infection sir, as one would say, to
  serve—
LAUNCELOT: Indeed the short and the long is, I serve the Jew,
  and have a desire—as my father shall specify—
GOBBO: His master and he—saving your worship's reverence—
  are scarce cater cousins—
LAUNCELOT: To be brief, the very truth is that the Jew, having
  done me wrong, doth cause me—as my father, being I hope
  an old man, shall frutify unto you—   119
GOBBO: I have here a dish of doves that I would bestow upon
  your worship, and my suit is—
LAUNCELOT: In very brief, the suit is impertinent to myself, as
  your worship shall know by this honest old man, and though
  I say it, though old man, yet poor man, my father.
BASSANIO: One speak for both. What would you?

127   *defect*, i.e. effect.

130   *preferred*, recommended.
       preferment, promotion.

133   *old proverb*, 'The grace of God is gear enough', ultimately from
       2 *Corinthians*, xii. 9.
       parted, shared.

138–9 *livery . . . guarded*. Probably a Fool's long, green motley coat
       braided (guarded) with yellow.
141–2 *if . . . book*. Various suggestions have been made: (*a*) 'I' (l. 142)
       = 'he'; (*b*) 'if any' = 'no'; (*c*) A phrase such as 'I'll ne'er wear hair
       on my face more' has been lost after 'book'.
142   *table*, palm of the hand.
       swear . . . book, take an oath while holding a Bible.
143   *simple . . . life*. Launcelot mocks palmistry with a ludicrous fore-
       cast of his own good fortune.
       simple, straightforward.
145   *simple coming-in*, modest allowance.
146   *'scape . . . thrice . . . peril*. ?2 *Corinthians*, xi. 25–6.
146–7 *peril . . . feather-bed*, (*a*) escape the thin end of the wedge of
       matrimony, (*b*) an anti-climax in that a feather-bed has no edge.
148   *gear*, business. A typical Vice's phrase.
149   *twinkling*, i.e. of an eye.
151   *bestowed*, stowed on board ship.

LAUNCELOT: Serve you sir.

GOBBO: That is the very defect of the matter sir.

BASSANIO: I know thee well, thou hast obtained thy suit.
Shylock thy master spoke with me this day,
And hath preferred thee, if it be preferment   130
To leave a rich Jew's service, to become
The follower of so poor a gentleman.

LAUNCELOT: The old proverb is very well parted between my
master Shylock and you sir: you have the grace of God sir, and
he hath enough.

BASSANIO: Thou speak'st it well. Go father with thy son.
Take leave of thy old master, and inquire
My lodging out. Give him a livery
More guarded than his fellows'. See it done.   139

LAUNCELOT: Father in. I cannot get a service, no, I have ne'er
a tongue in my head. Well, if any man in Italy have a fairer
table which doth offer to swear upon a book, I shall have
good fortune. Go to, here's a simple line of life, here's a small
trifle of wives, alas, fifteen wives is nothing, eleven widows
and nine maids is a simple coming-in for one man; and then
to 'scape drowning thrice, and to be in peril of my life with
the edge of a feather-bed, here are simple scapes. Well, if
Fortune be a woman, she's a good wench for this gear. Father
come; I'll take my leave of the Jew in the twinkling.

                              [*Exeunt Launcelot and old Gobbo*

BASSANIO: I pray thee, good Leonardo, think on this.   150
These things being bought and orderly bestowed,
Return in haste, for I do feast tonight
My best-esteemed acquaintance; hie thee, go.

LEONARDO: My best endeavours shall be done herein.

                    Enter GRATIANO

GRATIANO: Where is your master?

LEONARDO: Yonder sir he walks.   [*Exit*

161   *rude*, outspoken. Is this a just criticism of Gratiano?

165   *liberal*, uncontrolled.
166   *allay*, moderate, restrain.
      modesty, discretion.

169– Is Gratiano serious, frivolous, earnest, irrepressible, mocking,
  77 lying, effervescent?
170   *habit*, appearance.

173   *grace*, i.e. before a meal.
174   *hat*. Hats were normally worn indoors.
175   *use . . . civility*, obey all the rules of politeness.
176   *studied*, practised.
      sad ostent, grave appearance.

178   How does Bassanio receive this—solemnly, with laughter
      cautiously, mock solemnly?
178, *bearing, bar*. The two words were similar in sound.
  179

GRATIANO: Signior Bassanio.

BASSANIO: Gratiano.

GRATIANO: I have a suit to you.

BASSANIO: You have obtained it.

GRATIANO: You must not deny me, I must go with you to Belmont.

BASSANIO: Why then you must. But hear thee Gratiano,   160
 Thou art too wild, too rude and bold of voice,
 Parts that become thee happily enough,
 And in such eyes as ours appear not faults,
 But where thou art not known, why there they show
 Something too liberal. Pray thee take pain
 To allay with some cold drops of modesty
 Thy skipping spirit, lest through thy wild behaviour
 I be misconstrued in the place I go to,
 And lose my hopes.

GRATIANO: Signior Bassanio, hear me: 169
 If I do not put on a sober habit,
 Talk with respect, and swear but now and then,
 Wear prayer-books in my pocket, look demurely,
 Nay more, while grace is saying hood mine eyes
 Thus with my hat, and sigh and say, 'amen';
 Use all the observance of civility
 Like one well studied in a sad ostent
 To please his grandam, never trust me more.

BASSANIO: Well, we shall see your bearing.

GRATIANO: Nay but I bar tonight, you shall not gauge me   179
 By what we do tonight.

BASSANIO: No that were pity.
 I would entreat you rather to put on
 Your boldest suit of mirth, for we have friends
 That purpose merriment. But fare you well,
 I have some business.

GRATIANO: And I must to Lorenzo and the rest.
 But we will visit you at supper-time.   [*Exeunt*

Venice

This is a stealthy, secret meeting in which Jessica takes the lead. They should enter accordingly.

1   *I . . . so.* A neat way of identifying Jessica as Shylock's daughter.
2   *merry devil.* According to Owst, *Literature and Pulpit,* p. 112, 514–515, many of the devils were merry and Puck-like in their antics.

10   *exhibit,* (*a*) inhibit, prohibit, (*b*) show, display, i.e. my tears show what my tongue would utter if sorrow would allow it.
11   *pagan,* (*a*) heathen, (*b*) woman of bad character.
     Is Launcelot's weeping exaggerated, vociferous, sincere, mock, subdued?
     Jessica is anxious not to be seen with Launcelot, and hustles him off the stage. Shylock is suspicious by nature. See II. v, 43.
15   *heinous,* hateful.

18   *manners,* way of life.
     What words fit Jessica: ashamed, guilty, anxious, agitated, sly, passionate, loving, sympathetic, deceitful, tormented?

SCENE THREE

Enter JESSICA *and* LAUNCELOT

JESSICA: I am sorry thou wilt leave my father so:
Our house is hell, and thou, a merry devil,
Didst rob it of some taste of tediousness.
But fare thee well, there is a ducat for thee;
And Launcelot, soon at supper shalt thou see
Lorenzo, who is thy new master's guest.
Give him this letter, do it secretly,
And so farewell: I would not have my father
See me in talk with thee.   9
LAUNCELOT: Adieu, tears exhibit my tongue. Most beautiful
pagan, most sweet Jew, if a Christian do not play the knave
and get thee, I am much deceived. But adieu: these foolish
drops do something drown my manly spirit. Adieu.
JESSICA: Farewell good Launcelot.   [*Exit Launcelot*
Alack, what heinous sin is it in me
To be ashamed to be my father's child.
But though I am a daughter to his blood,
I am not to his manners. O Lorenzo
If thou keep promise, I shall end this strife,
Become a Christian and thy loving wife.   [*Exit*

Venice

Lorenzo is arranging his plans in the face of some doubts and hesitations among the others. He should speak with urgency and conviction in order to persuade them.

1   *slink . . . supper-time.* A common practice. Some of the guests after eating slipped away, masked and dressed themselves in fancy costumes, returned heralded by drum and fife and accompanied by torch-bearers, joined in the dances.

      These lines together with the entry of Launcelot below so soon after he had left Jessica disclose the rapid planning of and preparations for, the elopement.

5   *spoke us,* bespoke, arranged for.

6   *quaintly ordered,* skilfully planned.

10   *An,* if.

      break up, i.e. the waxen seal on the letter.

10–11 *it . . . signify,* it appears that it will inform you.

12   *hand,* writing.

      fair, graceful, neat.

19   *Hold . . . this.* Lorenzo rewards Launcelot.

      gentle, noble.

22   *masque.* An amateur dramatic performance usually in a private house, in which the players wore masks. It contained music, poetry and dancing.

SCENE FOUR

Enter GRATIANO, LORENZO, SALERIO, *and* SOLANIO

LORENZO: Nay, we will slink away in supper-time,
Disguise us at my lodging and return,
All in an hour.
GRATIANO: We have not made good preparation.
SALERIO: We have not spoke us yet of torch-bearers.
SOLANIO: 'Tis vile unless it may be quaintly ordered,
And better in my mind not undertook.
LORENZO: 'Tis now but four o'clock, we have two hours
To furnish us.

Enter LAUNCELOT *with a letter*
Friend Launcelot what's the news?
LAUNCELOT: An it shall please you to break up this, it shall seem
to signify.   11
LORENZO: I know the hand. In faith 'tis a fair hand,
And whiter than the paper it writ on
Is the fair hand that writ.
GRATIANO: Love-news in faith.
LAUNCELOT: By your leave sir.
LORENZO: Whither goest thou?
LAUNCELOT: Marry sir to bid my old master the Jew to sup
tonight with my new master the Christian.
LORENZO: Hold here, take this. Tell gentle Jessica
I will not fail her; speak it privately.   20
Go gentlemen,   [*Exit Launcelot*
Will you prepare you for this masque tonight?
I am provided of a torch-bearer.

81

33-4 What qualities in Jessica cause Lorenzo to say this? Is it put in to offset her lack of filial duty?

34   *gentle,* (*a*) noble, (*b*) gentile.

35   *foot,* path.

36   *she,* i.e. misfortune.

37   *issue,* child.
     faithless, unbelieving.

What is Lorenzo's mood as he tells Gratiano of Jessica's letter: mercenary, rapturous, elated, ecstatic, excited, unprincipled, unscrupulous?

Venice

Launcelot is magnificent in his new motley. How should he enter? Any stage business?

1-5 What qualities is Shylock attributing (*a*) to Bassanio, (*b*) to himself?

3   *gormandize,* eat like a glutton. Launcelot thought differently (II. ii, 95-6).

6   *Why Jessica!* Fools were noted for their powerful lungs.

9   *bidding* (*a*) being told, (*b*) calling, proclaiming.

SALERIO: Ay marry, I'll be gone about it straight.

SOLANIO: And so will I.

LORENZO: Meet me and Gratiano
At Gratiano's lodging some hour hence.

SALERIO: 'Tis good we do so.   [*Exeunt Salerio and Solanio*

GRATIANO: Was not that letter from fair Jessica?

LORENZO: I must needs tell thee all. She hath directed
How I shall take her from her father's house,   30
What gold and jewels she is furnished with,
What page's suit she hath in readiness.
If e'er the Jew her father come to heaven,
It will be for his gentle daughter's sake.
And never dare misfortune cross her foot,
Unless she do it under this excuse,
That she is issue to a faithless Jew.
Come go with me, peruse this as thou goest.
Fair Jessica shall be my torch-bearer.   [*Exeunt*

SCENE FIVE

Enter SHYLOCK *and* LAUNCELOT

SHYLOCK: Well, thou shalt see, thy eyes shall be thy judge,
The difference of old Shylock and Bassanio—
What Jessica!—thou shalt not gormandize
As thou hast done with me—What Jessica!—
And sleep, and snore, and rend apparel out—
Why Jessica, I say!

LAUNCELOT: Why Jessica!

SHYLOCK: Who bids thee call? I do not bid thee call.

LAUNCELOT: Your worship was wont to tell me I could do
nothing without bidding.

12–13 *But . . . me.* What is the effect on Jessica of Shylock's hesitations?

13 *I . . . me.* This condemns either Shylock or Antonio and Bassanio
—which?

14–15 *But . . . Christian.* Shylock's mean hatred makes him change his
mind (I. iii, 29–32).

15 *prodigal.* Shylock's view of Bassanio with an echo of the New
Testament parable.

18 *dream . . . bags.* To dream of money was considered an omen of
ill-luck.

tonight, last night.

20 *reproach,* i.e. approach.

21 *so . . . his.* Shylock takes up Launcelot's malapropism with
ominous satisfaction.

22 *conspired,* i.e. not only to arrange a masque.

24 *nose . . . a-bleeding.* A bad omen.

Black Monday, Easter Monday, 14th April, 1360, so called because
it was so dark, foggy, and cold that in King Edward III's army
besieging Paris many men died on horseback with cold.

Launcelot ridicules Shylock's superstitions with a mock
astrologer's forewarning and a further 'confusion' of the Christian
calendar.

29 *wry-necked.* So called because the player turned his face away from
the instrument. Shylock has no 'music in his soul'. See V. i, 83–8.

fife, player of the fife.

32 *varnished,* painted, or wearing painted masks.

34 *shallow foppery,* trivial foolery.

35 *Jacob's staff. Genesis,* xxxii. 10. 'For with my staff I passed over this
Jordan; and now I am become two bands', i.e. he had become
prosperous.

42 *Jewes eye,* (a) your looking for him, (b) the saying, 'as dear as a
Jew's eye', refers to payments made in medieval times by Jews to
escape having an eye put out.

Enter JESSICA

JESSICA: Call you? What is your will?   10

SHYLOCK: I am bid forth to supper Jessica;
   There are my keys. But wherefore should I go?
   I am not bid for love, they flatter me.
   But yet I'll go in hate, to feed upon
   The prodigal Christian. Jessica my girl,
   Look to my house. I am right loath to go,
   There is some ill a-brewing towards my rest,
   For I did dream of money bags tonight.

LAUNCELOT: I beseech you sir, go, my young master doth
   expect your reproach.   20

SHYLOCK: So do I his.

LAUNCELOT: And they have conspired together—I will not say
   you shall see a masque, but if you do, then it was not for nothing that my nose fell a-bleeding on Black-Monday last, at six
   o'clock i' the morning, falling out that year on Ash-Wednesday
   was four year in th'afternoon.

SHYLOCK: What are there masques? Hear you me Jessica:
   Lock up my doors, and when you hear the drum
   And the vile squealing of the wry-necked fife,
   Clamber not you up to the casements then,   30
   Nor thrust your head into the public street
   To gaze on Christian fools with varnished faces.
   But stop my house's ears, I mean my casements,
   Let not the sound of shallow foppery enter
   My sober house. By Jacob's staff, I swear,
   I have no mind of feasting forth tonight.
   But I will go. Go you before me sirrah,
   Say I will come.

LAUNCELOT: I will go before sir. Mistress, look out at window
   for all this—   40
              There will come a Christian by
              Will be worth a Jewes' eye.   [*Exit*

43 *Hagar's offspring,* the gentile outcast, Ishmael, Abraham's son by his Egyptian slave, Hagar.

  This incident again is typical of the Vice though normally he gives the improved version himself.

45 *patch,* fool.

  kind, natural.

46 *profit,* usefulness, improvement.

46–7 *sleeps . . . wildcat,* i.e. because it prowled by night.

47 *drones.* It was believed that they sucked honey from the hive.

55–6 What value has this couplet?

The series of short scenes acted briskly without pause between them gives the effect of swift action leading to the climax of the elopement.

 Gratiano and Salerio should enter purposively searching for the penthouse.

1 *penthouse,* porch, or overhanging roof.

2–4 What reason is there for the delay in Jessica's appearance and hence Lorenzo's?

5–7 *O . . . unforfeited,* the doves which draw the chariot of the goddess of love are readier to take her to bless a betrothal than a marriage by arrangement.

  Another interpretation taking 'pigeons' to mean 'lovers' is possible.

7 *obliged faith,* faith bound by contract.

10 *untread,* retrace.

11 *tedious measures,* the intricate movements of horses when put through their paces in the 'manage'.

SHYLOCK: What says that fool of Hagar's offspring ha?
JESSICA: His words were, 'Farewell mistress', nothing else.
SHYLOCK: The patch is kind enough, but a huge feeder,
  Snail-slow in profit, and he sleeps by day
  More than the wildcat. Drones hive not with me,
  Therefore I part with him, and part with him
  To one that I would have him help to waste
  His borrowed purse. Well Jessica, go in—   50
  Perhaps I will return immediately—
  Do as I bid you, shut doors after you.
  Fast bind, fast find,
  A proverb never stale in thrifty mind.   [*Exit*
JESSICA: Farewell, and if my fortune be not crossed,
  I have a father, you a daughter lost.   [*Exit*

SCENE SIX

Enter the masquers GRATIANO *and* SALERIO

GRATIANO: This is the penthouse under which Lorenzo
  Desired us to make stand.
SALERIO: His hour is almost past.
GRATIANO: And it is marvel he out-dwells his hour,
  For lovers ever run before the clock.
SALERIO: O ten times faster Venus' pigeons fly
  To seal love's bonds new-made, than they are wont
  To keep obliged faith unforfeited.
GRATIANO: That ever holds: who riseth from a feast
  With that keen appetite that he sits down?
  Where is the horse that doth untread again   10
  His tedious measures with the unbated fire
  That he did pace them first? All things that are,

14   *younger*, younger son. *prodigal*, the prodigal (younger) son of the parable.

15   *scarfed*, adorned with flags.

16   *strumpet*, wanton.

17   *How . . . return*. The prodigal son wasted his substance in riotous living with loose women and returned starving to his father, *St. Luke* xv.

18   *over-weathered*, weather damaged.

      ribs, (a) of the prodigal, *(b)* of the ship.

      Has the mingling of the story of the Prodigal Son with the imagery of a ship any value to the course of the action?

21   *abode*, delay.

35   *exchange*, i.e. her woman's clothes for a boy's garments.

36   *love . . . blind*. Cupid, the god of love, was represented as blind.

37   *pretty*, charming, ingenuous.

41   *hold . . . shames, (a)* light up my shameful disguise as a boy, *(b)* do penance for by misdeeds.

42   *light*, shameful with a quibble on 'candle light'.

Are with more spirit chased than enjoyed.
How like a younger or a prodigal
The scarfed bark puts from her native bay,
Hugged and embraced by the strumpet wind.
How like the prodigal doth she return,
With over-weathered ribs and ragged sails,
Lean, rent, and beggared by the strumpet wind.

SALERIO: Here comes Lorenzo, more of this hereafter.   2

Enter LORENZO

LORENZO: Sweet friends, your patience for my long abode.
    Not I, but my affairs, have made you wait.
    When you shall please to play the thieves for wives
    I'll watch as long for you then. Approach.
    Here dwells my father Jew. Ho, who's within?

Enter JESSICA *above, in boy's clothes*

JESSICA: Who are you? Tell me for more certainty,
    Albeit I'll swear that I do know your tongue.
LORENZO: Lorenzo and thy love.
JESSICA: Lorenzo certain, and my love indeed,
    For who love I so much? And now who knows   30
    But you Lorenzo, whether I am yours?
LORENZO: Heaven and thy thoughts are witness that thou art.
JESSICA: Here, catch this casket, it is worth the pains.
    I am glad 'tis night, you do not look on me,
    For I am much ashamed of my exchange.
    But love is blind, and lovers cannot see
    The pretty follies that themselves commit,
    For if they could, Cupid himself would blush
    To see me thus transformed to a boy.
LORENZO: Descend, for you must be my torch-bearer.   40
JESSICA: What, must I hold a candle to my shames?
    They in themselves, good sooth, are too too light.

43 *office of discovery*, work (as a torch-bearer which brings me into the light).
44 *obscured*, (*a*) hidden in the dark, (*b*) disguised.
45 *garnish*, dress.

47 *close*, concealing.
   runaway, i.e. as well as Jessica. Darkness is stealing away.

50 *moe*, more.

51 *by . . . hood*, a mild oath. Gratiano may be wearing a hood as part of his disguise.
   gentle, (*a*) Gentile, (*b*) a nobly born lady.
52 *Beshrew*, 'confound'. A playful oath. Each of the three words describes a quality appropriate to each of the three souls which men were believed to possess. So Jessica's excellent and complete personality is the picture of her that Lorenzo will carry in his faithful soul.

58 How does Lorenzo greet her?

65 *presently*, at once.
   It has been suggested that the cancellation of the masque shows that Shakespeare changed his original plan, or that it is intended to give the impression of speed by hurrying the action.
   What words fit Jessica: sly, unreliable, tender, sensitive, unscrupulous, thievish, humble, generous, sincere, courageous, heartless?
   Do you agree with Lorenzo's praise of her?

Why, 'tis an office of discovery, love,
And I should be obscured.

LORENZO: So are you, sweet,
Even in the lovely garnish of a boy.
But come at once,
For the close night doth play the runaway,
And we are stayed for at Bassanio's feast.

JESSICA: I will make fast the doors, and gild myself
With some moe ducats, and be with you straight.   50

[*Exit above*

GRATIANO: Now, by my hood, a gentle and no Jew.

LORENZO: Beshrew me but I love her heartily,
For she is wise, if I can judge of her,
And fair she is, if that mine eyes be true,
And true she is, as she hath proved herself;
And therefore like herself, wise, fair, and true,
Shall she be placed in my constant soul.

Enter JESSICA *below*

What, art thou come? On gentlemen, away,
Our masquing mates by this time for us stay.

[*Exit with Jessica and Salerio*

Enter ANTONIO

ANTONIO: Who's there?   60

GRATIANO: Signior Antonio?

ANTONIO: Fie, fie Gratiano, where are all the rest?
'Tis nine o'clock, our friends all stay for you.
No masque tonight, the wind is come about;
Bassanio presently will go aboard.
I have sent twenty out to seek for you.

GRATIANO: I am glad on't, I desire no more delight.
Than to be under sail, and gone tonight.   [*Exeunt*

Belmont

Again a formal, ceremonial entry. There should be tension, suspense and pattern in Morocco's movements as he moves to the caskets and raises them for inspection.

Alternatively, should pages present them to him? Normally he should be forward for his soliloquy.

Does Portia stand or sit?

1   *discover,* reveal.

2   *several,* separate, individual.

8   *dull,* (*a*) dim, (*b*) blunt (not sharp).
     blunt, (*a*) base, (*b*) outspoken.

9   *fair advantages,* good profits or benefits.

20   *golden,* noble. Will not humble itself for what appears worthless 'gold' and 'dross' are 'noble' and 'base' metals respectively.

22   *virgin hue,* pure whiteness. The Elizabethans regarded silver as white.

25   *even,* balanced, unbiased.

26   *If . . . estimation,* if you are taken at your own estimate of your worth, or reckoned according to your reputation.

27   *enough,* highly.

SCENE SEVEN

Flourish Cornets. Enter PORTIA *with the* PRINCE OF MOROCCO *and their trains*

PORTIA: Go draw aside the curtains, and discover
  The several caskets to this noble prince.
  Now make your choice.
MOROCCO: The first of gold, who this inscription bears,
  'Who chooseth me shall gain what many men desire'.
  The second silver, which this promise carries,
  'Who chooseth me shall get as much as he deserves'.
  This third dull lead, with warning all as blunt,
  'Who chooseth me must give and hazard all he hath'.
  How shall I know if I do choose the right?   10
PORTIA: The one of them contains my picture Prince:
  If you choose that, then I am yours withal.
MOROCCO: Some god direct my judgement. Let me see,
  I will survey the inscriptions back again.
  What says this leaden casket?
  'Who chooseth me must give and hazard all he hath.'
  Must give—for what? For lead? Hazard for lead?
  This casket threatens. Men that hazard all
  Do it in hope of fair advantages.
  A golden mind stoops not to shows of dross,   20
  I'll then nor give nor hazard aught for lead.
  What says the silver with her virgin hue?
  'Who chooseth me shall get as much as he deserves.'
  As much as he deserves? Pause there Morocco,
  And weigh thy value with an even hand.
  If thou be'st rated by thy estimation,
  Thou dost deserve enough, and yet enough
  May not extend so far as to the lady.

29–30   *And . . . myself,* And yet to doubt that I deserve her would be a timid failure to believe in myself.

33   *graces,* i.e. of body.

36   *graved,* engraved.

40   *shrine,* image of a saint.
breathing, living. Strictly saints can only be saints after death. Lovers seeking their lady were frequently likened to pilgrims worshipping at the shrine of a saint.

41   *Hyrcanian deserts.* A province of Persia south of the Caspian Sea, formerly notorious for its wildness and as the home of tigers.
vasty, vast.

44   *ambitious head,* swelling wave-crests. The sea as it were rebels against the heavens.

46   *spirits,* gallants. Dover Wilson suggests a quibble since it was believed that 'spirits' could not travel easily across water.

50   *base,* i.e. lead is a 'base' metal.

51   *rib,* enclose. *cerecloth,* shroud.

53   *ten . . . gold.* Gold was then worth ten times as much as silver.

56–7   *coin . . . gold.* A gold coin worth ten shillings called the 'angel' bearing St. Michael fighting the dragon.

57   *insculped upon,* embossed, carved in relief.
    Morocco's long soliloquy shows that he does not look below the surface, he is deceived by appearances; in fact he relies on his senses and is misled by them. The lowest of the three human souls dominates his character and actions. He takes it for granted that he deserves Portia, he considers the leaden casket not worth his attention and not worthy of Portia, only gold is not beneath his rank and hence appropriate to Portia's qualities. The image he thinks worthy of Portia leads him astray.

59–61   How is the key given to Morocco—by Portia or by a servant?

And yet to be afeard of my deserving
Were but a weak disabling of myself. 30
As much as I deserve, why that's the lady.
I do in birth deserve her, and in fortunes,
In graces, and in qualities of breeding;
But more than these, in love I do deserve.
What if I strayed no further, but chose here?
Let's see once more this saying graved in gold:
'Who chooseth me shall gain what many men desire'.
Why that's the lady, all the world desires her.
From the four corners of the earth they come
To kiss this shrine, this mortal breathing saint. 40
The Hyrcanian deserts and the vasty wilds
Of wide Arabia are as throughfares now
For princes to come view fair Portia.
The watery kingdom, whose ambitious head
Spits in the face of heaven, is no bar
To stop the foreign spirits, but they come
As o'er a brook to see fair Portia.
One of these three contains her heavenly picture.
Is't like that lead contains her? 'Twere damnation
To think so base a thought; it were too gross 50
To rib her cerecloth in the obscure grave.
Or shall I think in silver she's immured,
Being ten times undervalued to tried gold?
O sinful thought, never so rich a gem
Was set in worse than gold. They have in England
A coin that bears the figure of an angel
Stamped in gold, but that's insculped upon;
But here an angel in a golden bed
Lies all within. Deliver me the key.
Here do I choose, and thrive I as I may. 60
PORTIA: There, take it Prince, and if my form lie there,
Then I am yours.   [*He unlocks the golden casket*

95

63   *carrion Death*, the skull of a skeleton.

68   *outside*, the gold of the casket. i.e. The quest for gold has brought death to many who were brave but unwise.

73   *suit is cold*, courtship is finished. 'cold', perhaps a metaphor from hunting, i.e. cold scent; suit = chase; 'cold' also = dead.

74–7   What effect are these rhymes intended to have?

75   *farewell . . . frost*. 'Farewell frost' was an old saying used on the departure of anything unpleasant. Morocco turns it round since he must of force accept his cold rejection.

77   *part*, depart.

78   *gentle riddance*, a courteous withdrawal.

79   *complexion*, colour and temperament. Four syllables.

Venice

This scene reports briefly the sailing of Bassanio, and Jessica's elopement but its most important work is to describe the actions and words of Shylock and Antonio. Both have lost a person dear to them; Shylock has lost treasure with Jessica, and Antonio has risked money and life with Bassanio; both are deliberately and pointedly contrasted.

Solanio and Salerio do not merely recount what both already know for the benefit of the audience. They have been startled by the turn of events, and are excitedly and perhaps amusedly talking over Shylock's extraordinary behaviour.

MOROCCO:　　　　O hell! what have we here?
　A carrion Death, within whose empty eye
　There is a written scroll. I'll read the writing.

　　　　'All that glisters is not gold,
　　　　Often have you heard that told.
　　　　Many a man his life hath sold
　　　　But my outside to behold.
　　　　Gilded tombs do worms infold.
　　　　Had you been as wise as bold,　　　　　　70
　　　　Young in limbs, in judgement old,
　　　　Your answer had not been inscrolled.
　　　　Fare you well, your suit is cold.'

　　　　Cold indeed, and labour lost.
　　　　Then farewell heat, and welcome frost.
　Portia adieu. I have too grieved a heart
　To take a tedious leave. Thus losers part.

[Exit with his train

PORTIA: A gentle riddance. Draw the curtains, go.
　Let all of his complexion choose me so.

[Exeunt

SCENE EIGHT

Enter SALERIO *and* SOLANIO

SALERIO: Why man, I saw Bassanio under sail,
　With him is Gratiano gone along;
　And in their ship I am sure Lorenzo is not.
SOLANIO: The villain Jew with outcries raised the duke,
　Who went with him to search Bassanio's ship.
SALERIO: He came too late, the ship was under sail.

12   *passion*, rage.
      Should Solanio mimic Shylock's speech and gestures or not?
13   *variable*, switching from one thing to another.
      Are ll. 15–24 to be treated as comedy or not? If they are, how
      will Solanio and Salerio show it?

19   *double ducats*, worth 13s. 4d., twice the value of the ordinary ducat.

25   *keep his day*, i.e. repay the loan by the appointed day.
      A remark prepared for by Shylock's suspicion (ll. 4–5) and his
      hatred of Christians (l. 16) and (I. iii, 3–7).
      What words describe Shylock's mood: miserly, frenzied,
      crazed, horrified, indignant, avaricious, abused, betrayed, shocked,
      justified, fatherly?
27   *reasoned*, talked.
28   *narrow seas*, English Channel.
29   *miscarried*, was lost. This hint of loss gives an ominous turn to
      Shylock's ravings.
30   *fraught*, laden.

39   *slubber*, spoil.

But there the duke was given to understand
That in a gondola were seen together
Lorenzo and his amorous Jessica.
Besides, Antonio certified the duke   10
They were not with Bassanio in his ship.

SOLANIO: I never heard a passion so confused,
So strange, outrageous, and so variable,
As the dog Jew did utter in the streets:
'My daughter! O my ducats! O my daughter!
Fled with a Christian! O my Christian ducats!
Justice! The law! My ducats, and my daughter!
A sealed bag, two sealed bags of ducats,
Of double ducats, stolen from me by my daughter,
And jewels, two stones, two rich and precious stones,   20
Stolen by my daughter. Justice! Find the girl!
She hath the stones upon her, and the ducats.'

SALERIO: Why, all the boys in Venice follow him,
Crying, his stones, his daughter, and his ducats.

SOLANIO: Let good Antonio look he keep his day
Or he shall pay for this.

SALERIO: Marry well remembered.
I reasoned with a Frenchman yesterday,
Who told me, in the narrow seas that part
The French and English, there miscarried
A vessel of our country richly fraught.   30
I thought upon Antonio when he told me,
And wished in silence that it were not his.

SOLANIO: You were best to tell Antonio what you hear,
Yet do not suddenly, for it may grieve him.

SALERIO: A kinder gentleman treads not the earth.
I saw Bassanio and Antonio part,
Bassanio told him he would make some speed
Of his return. He answered, 'Do not so,
Slubber not business for my sake Bassanio,

40   *stay . . . time,* wait until your business is complete.

42   *mind of love,* loving mind, or, love schemes (Dover Wilson).

4   *ostents,* expressions.

46   *there,* then.

48   *sensible,* sensitive, deeply felt.

52   *quicken,* enliven.
       embraced heaviness, the grief that he 'hugs to himself' (Arden).
       Is Antonio kind, maudlin, generous, weak, gentle, self-sacrificing, self-effacing, effeminate, loving?

Belmont

Nerissa and the servants hustle in. Arragon and Portia make a formal, ceremonial entry. The scene may be viewed allegorically with Arragon representing pride, perhaps intellectual pride. His name hints at arrogance, and pride was a known failing of Spaniards.

    See note on presentation at the beginning of II. i.

1   *straight,* immediately.

2   *ta'en his oath,* i.e. at the temple (II. i, 44).
       election, choice.
       presently, immediately.

But stay the very riping of the time; 40
And for the Jew's bond which he hath of me,
Let it not enter in your mind of love.
Be merry, and employ your chiefest thoughts
To courtship and such fair ostents of love
As shall conveniently become you there.'
And even there, his eye being big with tears,
Turning his face, he put his hand behind him,
And with affection wondrous sensible
He wrung Bassanio's hand; and so they parted.
SOLANIO: I think he only loves the world for him. 50
I pray thee let us go and find him out
And quicken his embraced heaviness
With some delight or other.
SALERIO: Do we so. [*Exeunt*

SCENE NINE

Enter NERISSA *and a servant*

NERISSA: Quick, quick I pray thee, draw the curtain straight.
The Prince of Arragon hath ta'en his oath,
And comes to his election presently.

Flourish Cornets. Enter the PRINCE OF ARRAGON,
PORTIA, *and their trains*

PORTIA: Behold, there stand the caskets, noble prince.
If you choose that wherein I am contained,
Straight shall our nuptial rites be solemnized;
But if you fail, without more speech my lord,
You must be gone from hence immediately.
ARRAGON: I am enjoined by oath to observe three things:

19   *And . . . me,* and by so swearing I have prepared myself.
       addressed, prepared.

19–20 *fortune . . . to,* good luck . . . to. He moves towards the caskets.
       See note at head of II. vii.

20ff. Arragon does avoid Morocco's failure to see below the surface
       (ll. 26–7), he is well aware of false appearances (ll. 39–49), but he
       fails to submit himself to the judgement he applies to others.

26   *By,* for.
       fool, foolish.

27   *fond,* foolish.

28   *martlet,* martin, a word also meaning a dupe or fool. A 'martlet'
       could mean a swift, but Shakespeare probably was aware that a
       swift does not build 'on the outward wall'.

30   *force . . . casualty,* exposed to danger from and in the pathway of,
       accidents.

32   *jump,* agree.

37   *go about,* try.

38   *cozen,* cheat.

39   *stamp,* hall-mark, seal.
       No one should try to cheat Fortune by taking for himself an
       honour without clearly earning it.

41   *estates,* positions in life.
       degrees, social rank.

42   *derived,* (*a*) obtained, (*b*) inherited.
       clear, unstained.

43   *purchased,* gained.
       wearer, possessor.

First, never to unfold to any one   10
Which casket 'twas I chose; next, if I fail
Of the right casket, never in my life
To woo a maid in way of marriage;
Lastly,
If I do fail in fortune of my choice,
Immediately to leave you and be gone.
PORTIA: To these injunctions every one doth swear
 That comes to hazard for my worthless self.
ARRAGON: And so have I addressed me—fortune now
 To my heart's hope. Gold, silver, and base lead.   20
 'Who chooseth me must give and hazard all he hath.'
 You shall look fairer ere I give or hazard.
 What says the golden chest? ha, let me see:
 'Who chooseth me shall gain what many men desire'.
 What many men desire—that 'many' may be meant
 By the fool multitude that choose by show,
 Not learning more than the fond eye doth teach,
 Which pries not to the interior, but, like the martlet,
 Builds in the weather on the outward wall,
 Even in the force and road of casualty.   30
 I will not choose what many men desire,
 Because I will not jump with common spirits,
 And rank me with the barbarous multitudes.
 Why then to thee thou silver treasure-house,
 Tell me once more what title thou dost bear:
 'Who chooseth me shall get as much as he deserves'.
 And well said too; for who shall go about
 To cozen fortune and be honourable
 Without the stamp of merit? Let none presume
 To wear an undeserved dignity.   40
 O that estates, degrees, and offices,
 Were not derived corruptly, and that clear honour
 Were purchased by the merit of the wearer.

44   *cover*, keep their hats on, i.e. be masters who are now servants (Arden).

47   *true . . . honour*, true descendants of the nobility.
48   *ruin*, (a) refuse, (b) those who have been ruined by.
       times, conditions of life.
49   *new-varnished*, i.e. like a freshly painted coat of arms.

51   *I . . . desert*, I will take it that I am deserving.
           Arragon, scornful of popular opinion, rejects the golden casket. Proud of his own worth, he exclaims against the corrupt way in which many obtain their position and honours. Finally he does what no true Elizabethan lover should do—assumes that he deserves Portia.
53   During this pause is Arragon—staring, shocked, still, gesticulating?
54-60 Any change in Arragon's tones?
54   *blinking idiot*, i.e. fool's head.
56   *How much*. Perhaps an ironic echo of ll. 44-7.

61-2   *To . . . natures*, i.e. to commit an offence and then to sit as a judge of it are two things that do not agree.

68   *I wis*, certainly.
69   *silvered o'er*, silver-haired and therefore of wise appearance.

71   *I . . . head*. Although as a husband you will be the head of the family, you will always have a fool's head.
72   *sped*, done for.

How many then should cover that stand bare?
How many be commanded that command?
How much low peasantry would then be gleaned
From the true seed of honour? and how much honour
Picked from the chaff and ruin of the times
To be new-varnished? Well, but to my choice.
'Who chooseth me shall get as much as he deserves.'   50
I will assume desert. Give me a key for this,
And instantly unlock my fortunes here.

[*He opens the silver casket*

PORTIA: Too long a pause for that which you find there.
ARRAGON: What's here? The portrait of a blinking idiot
Presenting me a schedule. I will read it.
How much unlike art thou to Portia.
How much unlike my hopes and my deservings.
'Who chooseth me shall have as much as he deserves.'
Did I deserve no more than a fool's head?
Is that my prize? Are my deserts no better?   60
PORTIA: To offend and judge are distinct offices
And of opposed natures.
ARRAGON: What is here?

    'The fire seven times tried this:
    Seven times tried that judgement is,
    That did never choose amiss.
    Some there be that shadows kiss,
    Such have but a shadow's bliss.
    There be fools alive I wis,
    Silvered o'er; and so was this.
    Take what wife you will to bed,
    I will ever be your head.   71
    So be gone, you are sped.'

78   *ruth*, grief (Sisson). Some editors prefer 'wroth' from the Folio and Quarto reading 'wroath'. 'Wroth', however, was a current spelling of 'ruth' (Arden).

       Do the rhymes show relief, mockery, the end of the episode or mark proverbial sayings?

80   *deliberate fools*, i.e. they spend too much time considering.

81   *they . . . lose*, they have just sufficient wisdom to lose by using it.

      wit, intelligence, wisdom.

83   *Hanging . . . destiny*. A popular proverb.

85   The servant enters hurriedly with impressive news.

      my lord. A playful reply, perhaps indicating Portia's relief, and perhaps in gentle mockery of an odd person.

89   *sensible*, apparent to the senses.

      regreets, greetings with gifts.

90   *commends*, compliments.

      breath, speech.

94   *costly*, lavish.

      In view of Portia's reply, ll. 96–8, how does the messenger speak: slowly, excitedly, briskly, enthusiastically, coldly, romantically? Is he pompous, affected, conceited, obtuse, foppish?

98   *high–day*, high-flown.

100   *post*, messenger. *mannerly*, courteously.

101   *Lord Love*, Cupid.

      Is this line an aside to the audience?

    Still more fool I shall appear
    By the time I linger here.
    With one fool's head I came to woo,
    But I go away with two.
    Sweet adieu. I'll keep my oath,
    Patiently to bear my ruth.

[Exeunt Arragon and train

PORTIA: Thus hath the candle singed the moth
  O these deliberate fools, when they do choose,   80
  They have the wisdom by their wit to lose.
NERISSA: The ancient saying is no heresy,
  Hanging and wiving goes by destiny.
PORTIA: Come draw the curtain Nerissa.

Enter a Servant

SERVANT: Where is my lady?
PORTIA: Here. What would my lord?
SERVANT: Madam, there is alighted at your gate
  A young Venetian, one that comes before
  To signify th'approaching of his lord;
  From whom he bringeth sensible regreets,
  To wit, besides commends and courteous breath,   90
  Gifts of rich value. Yet I have not seen
  So likely an ambassador of love.
  A day in April never came so sweet
  To show how costly summer was at hand,
  As this fore-spurrer comes before his lord.
PORTIA: No more I pray thee, I am half afeard
  Thou wilt say anon he is some kin to thee,
  Thou spend'st such high-day wit in praising him.
  Come come Nerissa, for I long to see
  Quick Cupid's post that comes so mannerly.   100
NERISSA: Bassanio, Lord Love if thy will it be.   *[Exeunt*

Venice

Where are Solanio and Salerio going when they meet: about some urgent business, out for a stroll, to keep this appointment? Accordingly how will they enter? (see l. 62). They speak in rapid, urgent prose in contrast with the verse of the preceeding and following scenes.

2   *it . . . unchecked,* it still continues without contradiction.

What effect is this topical reference likely to have on the audience?

5   *tall,* fine.

6   *gossip Report,* madam rumour.

8   *knapped,* nibbled.

9–10 *slips of prolixity,* lapses into long-windedness. Solanio then gives just such a lapse.

13   *full stop,* (*a*) finish your speech, (*b*) control your colt-like careering.

17   *betimes,* in good time.

17–18 *lest . . . prayer,* for fear the devil may thwart me before I have time to say 'Amen' to Salerio's wish.

In what mood is Shylock: resentful, vengeful, savage, irresponsible, implacable, spiteful, hostile? His entry should indicate his mood. Is he blaming the others for Jessica's elopement? His agitation probably makes him restless.

23   *wings,* i.e. page's clothes.

25   *fledge,* i.e. fledged, sufficiently feathered to fly.
     complexion, nature.

What words describe the attitude of Solanio and Salerio: cynical, indifferent, callous, jeering, boastful, complacent, malicious, contemptuous?

ACT THREE

SCENE ONE

Enter SOLANIO *and* SALERIO

SOLANIO: Now what news on the Rialto?

SALERIO: Why yet it lives there unchecked, that Antonio hath a ship of rich lading wrecked on the narrow seas; the Goodwins I think they call the place, a very dangerous flat, and fatal, where the carcases of many a tall ship lie buried, as they say, if my gossip Report be an honest woman of her word.

SOLANIO: I would she were as lying a gossip in that as ever knapped ginger, or made her neighbours believe she wept for the death of a third husband. But it is true, without any slips of prolixity, or crossing the plain highway of talk, that the good Antonio, the honest Antonio——O that I had a title good enough to keep his name company—   12

SALERIO: Come, the full stop.

SOLANIO: Ha, what sayest thou? Why, the end is, he hath lost a ship.

SALERIO: I would it might prove the end of his losses.

SOLANIO: Let me say 'amen' betimes, lest the devil cross my prayer, for here he comes in the likeness of a Jew.

Enter SHYLOCK

How now Shylock, what news among the merchants?

SHYLOCK: You knew, none so well, none so well as you, of my daughter's flight.   21

SALERIO: That's certain. I for my part knew the tailor that made the wings she flew withal.

SOLANIO: And Shylock for his own part knew the bird was fledged, and then it is the complexion of them all to leave the dam.

26   *damned,* a quibble on 'dam', mother.

27   *devil . . . judge,* (*a*) Shylock (See ll. 17–18), (*b*) Satan.

28   *My . . . blood,* i.e. my own child.

29   *carrion,* rotting flesh—a word of abuse. Solanio deliberately mis-interprets Shylock's words. In effect he says, 'It is disgusting that you should have desires that you cannot control at your age'.

33   *red wine,* i.e. Jessica's young red blood.
      rhenish, hock, a white wine, i.e. Shylock's old thin pale blood.

35   *match,* (*a*) bargain, (*b*) similarity between himself and Jessica (ll 32–4).

37   *smug,* trimly dressed, i.e. in contrast to the rags of a beggar.
      mart, market place.

39–40 *for . . . courtesy,* out of Christian charity.
      Is Shylock exaggerating here? If so, why?

      There are two main stages in this speech, ll. 44–7, ll. 47–58, each with its climax—'I am a Jew' and 'why revenge'. There are minor climaxes also to be emphasized. The speech should be delivered with speed, and so that the key-word 'revenge' which occurs four times is brought out finally with a fanatical cry.

48   *dimensions,* bodily frame (Arden).

56   *humility.* An ironic mention of one of the chief Christian virtues.
      Is Shylock's argument just, one-sided, incomplete, distorted, unshakeable, beside the point?
      Note the rising intensity and passion of this speech with its short, stabbing, repetitive sentences, its step by step identifying of the common humanity of Jew and Christian.
      Shylock has possibly advanced to the front of the stage and delivered some of his speech direct to the audience while Salerio and Solanio turn to the messenger and see Tubal.
      What are they doing during Shylock's speech—trying to ignore him, listening courteously, showing contemptuous amuse-ment?

SHYLOCK: She is damned for it.

SALERIO: That's certain, if the devil may be her judge.

SHYLOCK: My own flesh and blood to rebel.

SOLANIO: Out upon it old carrion, rebels it at these years?

SHYLOCK: I say my daughter is my flesh and blood.   30

SALERIO: There is more difference between thy flesh and hers, than between jet and ivory; more between your bloods, than there is between red wine and rhenish. But tell us, do you hear whether Antonio have had any loss at sea or no?

SHYLOCK: There I have another bad match, a bankrupt, a prodigal, who dare scarce show his head on the Rialto, a beggar, that was used to come so smug upon the mart. Let him look to his bond. He was wont to call me usurer, let him look to his bond. He was wont to lend money for a Christian courtesy, let him look to his bond.   40

SALERIO: Why I am sure, if he forfeit, thou wilt not take his flesh, what's that good for?

SHYLOCK: To bait fish withal. If it will feed nothing else, it will feed my revenge. He hath disgraced me, and hindered me half a million, laughed at my losses, mocked at my gains, scorned my nation, thwarted my bargains, cooled my friends, heated mine enemies, and what's his reason? I am a Jew. Hath not a Jew eyes? Hath not a Jew hands, organs, dimensions, senses, affections, passions? Fed with the same food, hurt with the same weapons, subject to the same diseases, healed by the same means, warmed and cooled by the same winter and summer, as a Christian is? If you prick us do we not bleed? If you tickle us do we not laugh? If you poison us do we not die? And if you wrong us shall we not revenge? If we are like you in the rest, we will resemble you in that. If a Jew wrong a Christian, what is his humility? Revenge. If a Christian wrong a Jew, what should his sufferance be by Christian example? Why revenge. The villany you teach me I will execute, and it shall go hard but I will better the instruction.   59

63-4　*be matched,* i.e. be found to match them.

69-80　The turmoil in Shylock's mind is shown by the quick change
　　　　of moods in this speech: resentment at his own ill-luck, dismay at
　　　　the expense, hatred against Jessica, and a desire for revenge.
70　　　*Frankfort.* Frankfort fair, lasting a fortnight, was held twice yearly.
　　　　curse. Possibly *Deuteronomy,* xxviii, 15-68.
72-5　*I would . . . coffin.* Is this an agonized outburst, a comic clash of
　　　　moods, as Shylock has afterthoughts about his treasure?
74　　　*hearsed,* in her tomb.

Enter a Servant

SERVANT: Gentlemen, my master Antonio is at his house, and
desires to speak with you both.

SALERIO: We have been up and down to seek him.

Enter TUBAL

SOLANIO: Here comes another of the tribe; a third cannot be
matched, unless the devil himself turn Jew.

[*Exeunt Solanio, Salerio, and Servant*

SHYLOCK: How now Tubal, what news from Genoa? Hast
thou found my daughter?

TUBAL: I often came where I did hear of her, but cannot find
her.   68

SHYLOCK: Why there, there, there, there, a diamond gone cost
me two thousand ducats in Frankfort. The curse never fell
upon our nation till now, I never felt it till now. Two thousand
ducats in that, and other precious, precious jewels. I would
my daughter were dead at my foot, and the jewels in her ear.
Would she were hearsed at my foot, and the ducats in her
coffin. No news of them? Why so—and I know not what's
spent in the search. Why thou loss upon loss. The thief gone
with so much, and so much to find the thief, and no satisfaction, no revenge, nor no ill luck stirring but what lights on
my shoulders, no sighs but of my breathing, no tears but of
my shedding.   80

TUBAL: Yes, other men have ill luck too. Antonio, as I heard in
Genoa—

SHYLOCK: What, what, what, ill luck, ill luck?

TUBAL: Hath an argosy cast away coming from Tripolis.

SHYLOCK: I thank God, I thank God. Is it true, is it true?

TUBAL: I spoke with some of the sailors that escaped the wreck.

SHYLOCK: I thank thee good Tubal, good news, good news!
Ha, ha! Heard in Genoa?   88

94   *break,* go bankrupt.

100   Is this sentiment meant to be grotesquely comic in suggesting that
      Shylock could ever have loved, to add to his motives for revenge,
      or to gain him sympathy from the audience?

101   *wilderness,* a vast number, i.e. a bad bargain.

      Is Tubal's alternation between Antonio and Jessica a deliberate
      torturing of Shylock which Tubal enjoys, is it meant to produce a
      comic result in Shylock's reactions, is it a dramatic device to link
      the bond story with a motive for revenge, or is Tubal attempting
      to console Shylock by balancing the bad news about Jessica with
      good news of Antonio's misfortunes?

      Is Tubal a comic character? Is he stolid, unimaginative, cunning,
      sadistic, indifferent, ponderous, alert, impassive?

103-7 Note the haste and urgency.

103   *fee me,* engage for me.

104   *officer,* i.e. a sheriff's officer who made arrests.

105-6 *make . . . merchandise,* drive what bargains (Arden).

Belmont

Another ceremonial entry but less formal than the others. Portia's speech
betrays her anxiety and her love for Bassanio. In the stress of love she
speaks impulsively and then draws back her words. How far is there
allegory here? Does Bassanio represent understanding?

4   *but . . . love.* A self-defensive untruth! How should it be spoken?

5   *would not,* do not wish.

6   *Hate . . . quality,* it is not hate that gives advice of such a kind.

8   *quality,* manner, kind.

TUBAL: Your daughter spent in Genoa, as I heard, one night fourscore ducats.

SHYLOCK: Thou stick'st a dagger in me. I shall never see my gold again. Fourscore ducats at a sitting, fourscore ducats.

TUBAL: There came divers of Antonio's creditors in my company to Venice, that swear he cannot choose but break.

SHYLOCK: I am very glad of it, I'll plague him, I'll torture him. I am glad of it.

TUBAL: One of them showed me a ring that he had of your daughter for a monkey.   98

SHYLOCK: Out upon her, thou torturest me Tubal. It was my turquoise, I had it of Leah when I was a bachelor. I would not have given it for a wilderness of monkeys.

TUBAL: But Antonio is certainly undone.

SHYLOCK: Nay, that's true, that's very true. Go Tubal, fee me an officer; bespeak him a fortnight before. I will have the heart of him if he forfeit, for were he out of Venice, I can make what merchandise I will. Go Tubal, and meet me at our synagogue. Go good Tubal, at our synagogue Tubal.   [*Exeunt*

SCENE TWO

Enter BASSANIO, PORTIA, GRATIANO, NERISSA, *and Attendants*

PORTIA: I pray you tarry, pause a day or two
Before you hazard, for in choosing wrong
I lose your company; therefore forbear awhile.
There's something tells me—but it is not love—
I would not lose you, and you know yourself
Hate counsels not in such a quality.

8   *yet . . . thought,* yet a maiden is proverbially silent and has only her thoughts. Portia checks herself.

9   *some . . . two.* A rapid increase since l. 1.

15   *o'erlooked,* bewitched.

16–17 *One . . . all yours.* How does Bassanio receive this confession?

18   *naughty,* wicked.
     Any stage business? i.e. Does Bassanio offer any show of love?

20   *though . . . not yours,* yours by the right of love, but not yours in reality.
     Prove it, if it prove.

21   *Let . . . I,* let fortune be damned for preventing it, not I (i.e. for being forsworn).

22   *peize,* delay or extend.

23   *eke it,* eke it out, increase it.

25   Any movement or gesture to emphasize his feeling?

29   *fear the enjoying,* afraid that I shall not enjoy. Portia and Bassanio in the tense bitter sweetness of their love take refuge in an elaborate word play on torture by rack. The rack was frequently used to force traitors to confess their treason.

35   *confess . . . live.* Perhaps Portia hesitates before 'live' for 'confess and hang' was the expected proverbial phrase.

But lest you should not understand me well—
And yet a maiden hath no tongue but thought—
I would detain you here some month or two
Before you venture for me. I could teach you   10
How to choose right, but I am then forsworn;
So will I never be, so may you miss me;
But if you do, you'll make me wish a sin,
That I had been forsworn. Beshrew your eyes,
They have o'erlooked me, and divided me;
One half of me is yours, the other half yours—
Mine own I would say, but if mine then yours,
And so all yours. O these naughty times
Put bars between the owners and their rights.
And so though yours, not yours. Prove it so.   20
Let fortune go to hell for it, not I.
I speak too long, but 'tis to peize the time,
To eke it, and to draw it out in length,
To stay you from election.

BASSANIO: Let me choose,
For as I am, I live upon the rack.

PORTIA: Upon the rack Bassanio then confess
What treason there is mingled with your love.

BASSANIO: None but that ugly treason of mistrust,
Which makes me fear the enjoying of my love.
There may as well be amity and life   30
'Tween snow and fire, as treason and my love.

PORTIA: Ay but I fear you speak upon the rack
Where men enforced do speak anything.

BASSANIO: Promise me life, and I'll confess the truth.

PORTIA: Well then, confess and live.

BASSANIO: 'Confess' and 'love'
Had been the very sum of my confession.
O happy torment, when my torturer
Doth teach me answers for deliverance.

40   *Away then.* Any gesture and movement?

41   *If . . . out,* i.e. If your love is true it will guide you to me.

42   *stand . . . aloof.* Dover Wilson suggests that they join the musicians in the gallery ready for the song in which all join. The audience's attention is thus concentrated on Bassanio and Portia.

44–62   Portia is no longer addressing Bassanio; these lines are an 'aside' to the audience, the quick succession of similes reveals her emotion as she comments on Bassanio's approach to the caskets. The first thirteen lines of Portia's speech cover the withdrawal of the attendants and the drawing back of the curtains to reveal the caskets.

44–5   *swan-like . . . music.* According to a classical myth swans, normally mute, sang very sweetly when they were dying.

46   *proper,* correct, apt. A rhetorical term.

46–7   *my eye . . . death-bed,* i.e. in her tears.

        What different moods is Portia expressing in ll. 44–7 and in ll. 47–53? How can her speaking help to show this?

51–3   *dulcet . . . marriage.* It was an old custom to wake the bridegroom on his wedding morning by playing music under his window.

53   *Now . . .* Any movement, gesture by Portia, or change in the speed or pitch of her utterance?

54   *presence,* dignity, noble appearance.

        much . . . love. According to a story told by Ovid, Hercules (Alcides) rescued Hesione, daughter of Laomedon, King of Troy, from a sea-monster to which she had been offered as a sacrifice. Hercules was not in love with Hesione, he had been promised a gift of horses as a reward.

56   *virgin tribute,* Hesione.

57   *I . . . sacrifice,* i.e. like Hesione. Is there perhaps a deeper suggestion here apparent when Portia is admitted to the trial immediately after Shylock's claim 'I stand for judgement' (IV. i, 103)? Portia speaks emphatically.

58   *The rest,* Nerissa and attendants.

        Dardanian, Trojan.

59   *bleared,* tear-stained.

60   *issue,* result.

63   *fancy,* light-hearted attraction, surface love.

        Opinion is divided about the purpose of this song. Some think that its rhymes with 'lead', its dirge-like form and its reference to death implying a leaden coffin, hint to Bassanio which casket to

But let me to my fortune and the caskets.
PORTIA: Away then, I am locked in one of them,   40
If you do love me, you will find me out.
Nerissa and the rest, stand all aloof,
Let music sound while he doth make his choice;
Then if he lose he makes a swan-like end,
Fading in music. That the comparison
May stand more proper, my eye shall be the stream
And watery death-bed for him. He may win,
And what is music then? Then music is
Even as the flourish, when true subjects bow
To a new-crowned monarch. Such it is   50
As are those dulcet sounds in break of day
That creep into the dreaming bridegroom's ear
And summon him to marriage. Now he goes
With no less presence, but with much more love,
Than young Alcides, when he did redeem
The virgin tribute paid by howling Troy
To the sea-monster. I stand for sacrifice;
The rest aloof are the Dardanian wives,
With bleared visages come forth to view
The issue of th'exploit. Go Hercules.   60
Live thou, I live. With much much more dismay
I view the fight than thou that mak'st the fray.

A song to music the whilst BASSANIO *comments on the caskets
to himself*

Tell me where is fancy bred,
Or in the heart or in the head?
How begot, how nourished?

choose. Moreover, in folk stories of this kind the successful lover is usually helped by some person or by some charm. Bassanio's first words may show that he has taken the hint, because he speaks out of character.

Others claim that Portia who has declared that she will not help Bassanio (ll. 10–12), who relies on the lottery entirely (l. 41) and who is of too high an integrity to cheat would not even indirectly have given Bassanio a clue. The stage direction 'A song the whilst Bassanio comments on the caskets to himself' is almost certainly Shakespeare's, and 'to himself' suggests that he ignores the song.

Perhaps it is best to assume that the song underlines the intense emotional climax of the casket theme, that it reminds the audience that the choice is a test of true love in the presence of which light, superficial love quickly dies, and that it is a chorus comment to the audience foreshadowing Bassanio's thoughts but independent of them.

J. Long, *Shakespeare's Use of Music,* suggests that the soloist accompanied himself and the chorus with a lute.

74   *still,* continually.
75, 76 *tainted—corrupt—seasoned.* Note the underlying metaphor.
78   *damned error,* heresy. A belief that will lead to damnation.
        sober brow, grave scholar.
79   *approve,* justify.
81   *simple,* wholly vicious.
85   *Mars.* The Roman god of war.
86   *livers . . . milk.* The liver was supposed to be the seat of courage. Cold blood (i.e. cowardice) left the liver pale and white.
87   *valour's excrement,* a hero's beard. *excrement,* outgrowth (usually of hair).
88   *redoubted,* feared.
88–91   *Look . . . it,* If you examine a woman's beautiful appearance, you will see that it is made up from cosmetics bought by weight. This works a miracle against the laws of nature, for those with the greatest weight (of cosmetics) are the lightest (in character).
90   *miracle in nature,* (a) an overturning of the laws of nature, (b) a beautifying of those who were plain.
92   *crisped,* curly.
        snakey, (a) flowing, (b) treacherous.
93   *wanton,* alluring.
94   *upon . . . fairness,* on a head made beautiful artificially.
95   *dowry,* gift, legacy.

ALL: Reply, reply.

             It is engendered in the eyes,
             With gazing fed; and fancy dies
             In the cradle where it lies.
                 Let us all ring fancy's knell;   70
                 I'll begin it, ding, dong, bell.

ALL: Ding, dong, bell.

BASSANIO: So may the outward shows be least themselves.
The world is still deceived with ornament.
In law, what plea so tainted and corrupt
But being seasoned with a gracious voice,
Obscures the show of evil? In religion,
What damned error but some sober brow
Will bless it, and approve it with a text,
Hiding the grossness with fair ornament?   80
There is no vice so simple, but assumes
Some mark of virtue on his outward parts.
How many cowards whose hearts are all as false
As stairs of sand, wear yet upon their chins
The beards of Hercules and frowning Mars,
Who inward searched, have livers white as milk?
And these assume but valour's excrement
To render them redoubted. Look on beauty,
And you shall see 'tis purchased by the weight,
Which therein works a miracle in nature,   90
Making them lightest that wear most of it.
So are those crisped snaky golden locks
Which make such wanton gambols with the wind
Upon supposed fairness, often known
To be the dowry of a second head,

96   *in,* i.e. being in.

97   *guiled,* treacherous.

99   *Indian beauty.* Ironic. The Elizabethans despised dark hair and swarthy complexions. Which word should be emphasized?

100   *times,* opportunities.

102   *Hard . . . Midas.* In classical legend Midas, king of Phrygia, was endowed by the god Dionysius with the power to turn anything he touched to gold. As it was impossible for him to eat, since his food turned to gold, he begged the god to take the gift from him.

103   *palled,* stale. Some editors prefer 'pale' from the quarto and folio editions, but it is odd that Bassanio should reject the paleness of silver but approve the paleness of lead (l. 106).

      common drudge, i.e. as coins it would be everybody's servant. Should Bassanio lift up and examine the caskets as he is speaking? Where is Portia (l. 109 gives a clue) and what is she doing during the speech? Is she standing, sitting, moving, motionless? Is she tense, politely interested, approving, rapt, restless?

107   *And . . . consequence.* Any gesture or movement? How does Portia react? Should Bassanio receive a key, or is this deliberately omitted to avoid disturbing the movement of the scene?

110   *jealousy,* mistrust.

112   *measure,* moderation.

      scant, lessen. *excess,* (*a*) overplus of happiness, (*b*) love's usury (See I. iii, 56).

115   *counterfeit,* picture, likeness.

115   A lover was expected to praise his lady's beauty. So far, Bassanio, apart from his brief account to Antonio, has not done so—a most discourteous omission. Portia's portrait now gives him the opportunity of paying the devoted lover's compliment to his lady.

      The general trend of the speech is not unlike that of a sonnet. After praising her pictured beauty in detail Bassanio then asserts how far short the painting is by comparison with the real Portia. (Compare Spenser, *Amoretti,* XVII). It also continues in a different way the contrast of appearance with reality in his previous speech.

      Portia may move slowly towards him during this speech.

116   *Hath . . . creation,* has made a painting so true to life.

118   *severed,* parted, half-open.

124–6 Portia's eyes were so bright that, having painted one, the painter would be dazzled and unable to complete the other.

The skull that bred them in the sepulchre.
Thus ornament is but the guiled shore
To a most dangerous sea, the beauteous scarf
Veiling an Indian beauty; in a word,
The seeming truth which cunning times put on   100
To entrap the wisest. Therefore thou gaudy gold,
Hard food for Midas, I will none of thee.
Nor none of thee, thou palled and common drudge
'Tween man and man. But thou, thou meagre lead
Which rather threatenest than dost promise aught,
Thy paleness moves me more than eloquence,
And here choose I, joy be the consequence.

PORTIA: [*Aside*] How all the other passions fleet to air,
As doubtful thoughts, and rash-embraced despair,
And shuddering fear, and green-eyed jealousy.   110
O love be moderate, allay thy ecstasy,
In measure rain thy joy, scant this excess.
I feel too much thy blessing, make it less
For fear I surfeit.

BASSANIO: What find I here?

[*He opens the leaden casket*

Fair Portia's counterfeit. What demi-god
Hath come so near creation? Move these eyes?
Or whether riding on the balls of mine
Seem they in motion? Here are severed lips
Parted with sugar breath, so sweet a bar
Should sunder such sweet friends. Here in her hairs   120
The painter plays the spider, and hath woven
A golden mesh t'entrap the hearts of men
Faster than gnats in cobwebs: but her eyes—
How could he see to do them? Having made one,
Methinks it should have power to steal both his

126   *unfurnished*, i.e. with its fellow eye.

127   *substance*, amount, gist.
      shadow, picture.

129   *substance*, original (Portia). A quibble with the previous 'substance'.
      The arrangement of words substance—shadow, shadow—sub-
      stance, was a common rhetorical practice.

130   *continent*, that which contains.

139–   Why does Bassanio suddenly speak in rhyme?
48

140   *by note*, i.e. a bill, an account of what is owing, with a quibble on
      the usual meaning of note.
      receive. Does Bassanio kiss Portia here or later? If so, how? Timing
      and technique are important to obtain the suggestion of a first
      wonderful, yet respectful and dignified, kiss.

148   The image of 'note' is extended by other terms used in com-
      merce.

149–   These lines are a lovely committal to marriage, they anticipate the
72   wedding ceremony.

156   *account*, esteem, opinion.

157   *livings*, possessions.

And leave itself unfurnished. Yet look how far
The substance of my praise doth wrong this shadow
In underprizing it, so far this shadow
Doth limp behind the substance. Here's the scroll,
The continent and summary of my fortune.   130

      'You that choose not by the view,
      Chance as fair and choose as true.
      Since this fortune falls to you,
      Be content and seek no new.
      If you be well pleased with this
      And hold your fortune for your bliss,
      Turn you where your lady is,
      And claim her with a loving kiss.'

A gentle scroll. Fair lady, by your leave.
I come by note to give, and to receive.   140
Like one of two contending in a prize
That thinks he hath done well in people's eyes,
Hearing applause and universal shout,
Giddy in spirit, still gazing in a doubt
Whether those peals of praise be his or no,
So thrice-fair lady stand I even so,
As doubtful whether what I see be true,
Until confirmed, signed, ratified by you.
PORTIA: You see me Lord Bassanio where I stand,
Such as I am. Though for myself alone   150
I would not be ambitious in my wish,
To wish myself much better, yet for you,
I would be trebled twenty times myself,
A thousand times more fair, ten thousand times
More rich,
That only to stand high in your account,
I might in virtues, beauties, livings, friends,

158   *account,* enumeration.

159   *sum of nothing.* This is the Folio version. Some editors prefer the Quarto reading 'sum (or 'some') of something'. Portia, however follows it by three negatives or nothings: 'unlessoned, unschooled, unpractised'.

      term in gross, give in full. A commercial phrase.

160   *unpractised,* unaccomplished.

      This speech is carefully constructed with terms arranged in threes, some of them interrelated. Its apparent simplicity is in keeping with Portia's serene, humble sincerity and frankness.

      In the courtesy books of the period it is laid down that a husband's duty is to instruct his wife in her proper attitude to him as her superior, in the managing of his house to his satisfaction, and in religious and moral duties. By marriage a woman gives herself and her dowry to her husband and regards him very much as a vassal regards his king (R. Kelso, *Doctrine for the Lady of the Renaissance,* pp. 83–4).

168   *converted.* Another commercial term.

170   *even now* . . . now, even now, at this very moment.

172   *my lord's.* Any movement?

175   *vantage,* opportunity, privilege.

      exclaim on, accuse, reproach.

      Nerissa and Gratiano may return to the stage about this point.

177–8   *Only . . . powers.* Blood was supposed to carry the spirits which controlled the emotions, and were the means of communication between the senses and the soul.

182–4   *powers,* i.e. of mind and body.

      Where all recognizable utterances are mingled and become a widespread confusion expressing nothing distinctly except a general rejoicing.

Exceed account. But the full sum of me
Is sum of nothing; which to term in gross,
Is an unlessoned girl, unschooled, unpractised,   160
Happy in this, she is not yet so old
But she may learn; happier than this,
She is not bred so dull but she can learn;
Happiest of all, is that her gentle spirit
Commits itself to yours to be directed,
As from her lord, her governor, her king.
Myself, and what is mine, to you and yours
Is now converted. But now I was the lord
Of this fair mansion, master of my servants,
Queen o'er myself. And even now, but now,   170
This house, these servants and this same myself
Are yours my lord's—I give them with this ring,
Which when you part from, lose, or give away,
Let it presage the ruin of your love,
And be my vantage to exclaim on you.
BASSANIO: Madam, you have bereft me of all words,
Only my blood speaks to you in my veins,
And there is such confusion in my powers,
As after some oration fairly spoke
By a beloved prince, there doth appear   180
Among the buzzing pleased multitude,
Where every something, being blent together,
Turns to a wild of nothing, save of joy
Expressed, and not expressed. But when this ring
Parts from this finger, then parts life from hence:
O then be bold to say Bassanio's dead.
NERISSA: My lord and lady, it is now our time
That have stood by and seen our wishes prosper,
To cry good joy, good joy my lord and lady.
GRATIANO: My lord Bassanio and my gentle lady,   190
I wish you all the joy that you can wish,

192   *none . . . me*, i.e. no more than I wish you (Arden).

196–   Gratiano's wooing is a deliberate contrast with that of Bassanio.
 209   Its flippant, swaggering tone gives a touch of comedy before the
        news of Antonio's disaster.

200–1   *for . . . you*, for it is not my habit to delay any more than it is
        yours.

205   *roof*, i.e. of his mouth.

214   *play . . . boy*. We will bet a thousand ducats we will have a son
        before they do.

219   *infidel*, i.e. Jessica.

For I am sure you can wish none from me.
And when your honours mean to solemnize
The bargain of your faith, I do beseech you
Even at that time I may be married too.
BASSANIO: With all my heart, so thou canst get a wife.
GRATIANO: I thank your lordship, you have got me one.
My eyes my lord can look as swift as yours.
You saw the mistress, I beheld the maid.
You loved, I loved, for intermission   200
No more pertains to me my lord than you.
Your fortune stood upon the casket there,
And so did mine too as the matter falls.
For wooing here until I sweat again,
And swearing till my very roof was dry
With oaths of love, at last, if promise last,
I got a promise of this fair one here
To have her love, provided that your fortune
Achieved her mistress.
PORTIA: Is this true Nerissa?
NERISSA: Madam it is, so you stand pleased withal.   210
BASSANIO: And do you Gratiano mean good faith?
GRATIANO: Yes faith my lord.
BASSANIO: Our feast shall be much honoured in your marriage.
GRATIANO: We'll play with them the first boy for a thousand
    ducats.
NERISSA: What, and stake down?
GRATIANO: No, we shall ne'er win at that sport, and stake
    down.
BASSANIO: But who comes here? Lorenzo and his infidel?
What, and my old Venetian friend Salerio?   220

Enter LORENZO, JESSICA, *and* SALERIO, *a Messenger
from Venice*

BASSANIO: Lorenzo and Salerio, welcome hither,

222 *youth . . . interest,* if my position here, so newly gained, gives me
authority to welcome you.

Portia gracefully admits Bassanio's authority and gives a general
welcome to the new-comers. Many of the greetings will be in
gesture and movement.

224 *very,* true.

233 *commends . . . you,* wishes to be remembered to you.

Salerio says that Antonio is not suffering from a bodily disease
but that his health depends on his attitude of mind.

237 *estate,* state.

Jessica had remained in the background—why?

238 Bassanio goes aside.

240 *royal,* princely, noblest.

242 *we . . . fleece.* Gratiano is joyfully exulting in marked contrast with
Salerio's grave demeanour.

243 *fleece.* Perhaps a pun on 'fleets'.

244 *shrewd contents,* i.e. bad news. *shrewd,* hurtful, evil.

247–8 *turn . . . man,* so deeply upset the composure of any self-possessed
man.

Some stage business is required from Portia and Bassanio during
this speech. What movements would be appropriate? At l. 249
she presumably moves to him.

If that the youth of my new interest here
Have power to bid you welcome. By your leave,
I bid my very friends and countrymen,
Sweet Portia, welcome,

PORTIA: So do I my lord,
They are entirely welcome.

LORENZO: I thank your honour. For my part my lord,
My purpose was not to have seen you here,
But meeting with Salerio by the way
He did intreat me past all saying nay   230
To come with him along.

SALERIO: I did my lord,
And I have reason for it. Signior Antonio
Commends him to you.   [*Gives Bassanio a letter*

BASSANIO: Ere I ope his letter
I pray you tell me how my good friend doth.

SALERIO: Not sick my lord, unless it be in mind,
Nor well, unless in mind. His letter there
Will show you his estate.   [*Bassanio opens the letter*

GRATIANO: Nerissa, cheer yond stranger, bid her welcome.
Your hand Salerio, what's the news from Venice?
How doth that royal merchant, good Antonio?   240
I know he will be glad of our success.
We are the Jasons, we have won the fleece.

SALERIO: I would you had won the fleece that he hath lost.

PORTIA: There are some shrewd contents in yond same paper
That steals the colour from Bassanio's cheek.
Some dear friend dead, else nothing in the world
Could turn so much the constitution
Of any constant man. What, worse and worse?
With leave Bassanio, I am half yourself,
And I must freely have the half of anything   250
That this same paper brings you.

BASSANIO: O sweet Portia,

258–   *Rating . . . than nothing.* Bassanio and Portia in parallel humble
   61   themselves to each other as worth nothing, and both enrich
        their character by so doing.
260   *state*, estate.

262   *engaged*, pledged, bound.
263   *mere*, absolute.
264   *feed . . . means*, supply me with the means (to woo you).
        Are these words extravagant and far fetched or are they the
        expression of an anguished and tortured mind? Accordingly how
        should they be uttered?

268   *hit*, success.

272   *merchant*, merchant ship.
272–   How are these statements received by (*a*) Bassanio, (*b*) Portia, (*c*)
   91 Gratiano and the others?

274   *present*, ready.
        discharge, pay.

277   *keen*, cruel.
        confound, destroy.

279–   *impeach . . . justice*, if he is denied justice he will bring charges
   80 against the city for breaking the terms of its charter of freedom.
281   *magnificoes*, chief men.
282   *port*, rank.
        persuaded, pleaded.
283   *envious*, hateful, malicious.

Here are a few of the unpleasant'st words
That ever blotted paper. Gentle lady,
When I did first impart my love to you,
I freely told you all the wealth I had
Ran in my veins—I was a gentleman,
And then I told you true. And yet dear lady,
Rating myself at nothing, you shall see
How much I was a braggart. When I told you
My state was nothing, I should then have told you   260
That I was worse than nothing; for indeed
I have engaged myself to a dear friend,
Engaged my friend to his mere enemy
To feed my means. Here is a letter lady;
The paper as the body of my friend,
And every word in it a gaping wound
Issuing life-blood. But is it true Salerio?
Have all his ventures failed? What not one hit?
From Tripolis, from Mexico and England,
From Lisbon, Barbary and India?   270
And not one vessel 'scape the dreadful touch
Of merchant-marring rocks?

SALERIO: Not one my lord.
Besides, it should appear, that if he had
The present money to discharge the Jew,
He would not take it. Never did I know
A creature that did bear the shape of man
So keen and greedy to confound a man.
He plies the duke at morning and at night,
And doth impeach the freedom of the state
If they dêny him justice. Twenty merchants,   280
The duke himself, and the magnificoes
Of greatest port have all persuaded with him,
But none can drive him from the envious plea
Of forfeiture, of justice, and his bond.

What effect is Jessica's speech likely to have on the audience?

294 *best-conditioned*, best-natured.

294–5 *unwearied . . . courtesies.* See III. i, 44. An echo of *Galatians*, vi. 9 (compare 2 *Thessalonians*, iii. 13), 'And let us not be weary in well doing'.

296 *ancient . . . honour*, uprightness and a high sense of duty.

300 *deface*, cancel.

303 *fault*, failure.

313 *cheer*, face, mood.

314 *dear.* Is this pun an attempt to lighten Bassanio's sadness or a 'joyful acknowledgment of the pleasure of giving for love' (Arden)?

  The first part of the letter is already known to the audience, the second part, 'and since . . .', with Antonio's moving plea to have his friend's presence and support at his death, brings his peril with startling urgency before them. It also presents the sharp challenge of friendship to the newly established love of Bassanio.

  Portia is indeed loving and giving, generous, self-sacrificing and magnanimous.

  The four lines of rhymed verse set a solemn seal on Bassanio's promise.

JESSICA: When I was with him, I have heard him swear
    To Tubal and to Chus, his countrymen,
    That he would rather have Antonio's flesh
    Than twenty times the value of the sum
    That he did owe him. And I know my lord,
    If law, authority, and power deny not,   290
    It will go hard with poor Antonio.
PORTIA: Is it your dear friend that is thus in trouble?
BASSANIO: The dearest friend to me, the kindest man,
    The best-conditioned and unwearied spirit
    In doing courtesies; and one in whom
    The ancient Roman honour more appears
    Than any that draws breath in Italy.
PORTIA: What sum owes he the Jew?
BASSANIO: For me three thousand ducats.
PORTIA: What, no more?
    Pay him six thousand, and deface the bond;   300
    Double six thousand, and then treble that,
    Before a friend of this description
    Shall lose a hair through Bassanio's fault.
    First go with me to church, and call me wife,
    And then away to Venice to your friend.
    For never shall you lie by Portia's side
    With an unquiet soul. You shall have gold
    To pay the petty debt twenty times over.
    When it is paid, bring your true friend along.
    My maid Nerissa and myself meantime   310
    Will live as maids and widows. Come away.
    For you shall hence upon your wedding-day.
    Bid your friends welcome, show a merry cheer,
    Since you are dear bought, I will love you dear.
    But let me hear the letter of your friend.
BASSANIO: [*Reads*] Sweet Bassanio, my ships have all miscarried,
    my creditors grow cruel, my estate is very low, my bond to

Venice

This scene contains a personal plea by Antonio to Shylock which the latter refuses to hear, Shylock's unrelenting insistence on his bond, a further account of Shylock's murderous hatred and of the impossibility of changing the course of law.

Dramatically bringing Antonio and Shylock face to face increases the urgency and tension, and the sense of inevitable doom closing rapidly on Antonio. Although Bassanio provided with money is hastening to rescue Antonio, his endeavour, in view of Shylock's merciless determination, seems bound to fail.

How do they enter?

1   *tell . . . mercy.* Has Shylock come to rail at Antonio or is Antonio looking for Shylock?

       What does this imply?

9   *naughty,* worthless, wicked.
     fond, foolish, lenient.

14   *dull-eyed,* gullible, easily tricked.

16   *Christian intercessors.* Spoken with sarcasm. The word 'intercessor' was closely associated with Christ.

the Jew is forfeit, and since in paying it, it is impossible I should live, all debts are cleared between you and I if I might but see you at my death. Notwithstanding, use your pleasure; if your love do not persuade you to come, let not my letter.   321

PORTIA: O love, dispatch all business and be gone.

BASSANIO: Since I have your good leave to go away,
          I will make haste; but till I come again,
          No bed shall e'er be guilty of my stay,
          No rest be interposer 'twixt us twain.   *[Exeunt*

SCENE THREE

Enter SHYLOCK, SOLANIO, ANTONIO, *and Gaoler*

SHYLOCK: Gaoler, look to him, tell not me of mercy,
  This is the fool that lent out money gratis.
  Gaoler, look to him.

ANTONIO: Hear me yet good Shylock.

SHYLOCK: I'll have my bond, speak not against my bond,
  I have sworn an oath that I will have my bond.
  Thou call'dst me dog before thou hadst a cause,
  But since I am a dog, beware my fangs.
  The duke shall grant me justice. I do wonder,
  Thou naughty gaoler, that thou art so fond
  To come abroad with him at his request.   10

ANTONIO: I pray thee hear me speak.

SHYLOCK: I'll have my bond. I will not hear thee speak.
  I'll have my bond, and therefore speak no more.
  I'll not be made a soft and dull-eyed fool,
  To shake the head, relent, and sigh, and yield
  To Christian intercessors. Follow not;
  I'll have no speaking. I will have my bond.   *[Exit*

18   *impenetrable,* hard-hearted.

20   *bootless prayers,* unsuccessful requests.

22–3   *I . . . me.* A fresh aspect of the relations between Antonio and Shylock.
        What purpose does this serve?

25   *grant . . . hold,* allow . . . stand.

27   *commodity,* benefits, privileges.

29   *impeach,* cast doubt upon.

32   *bated me,* (*a*) caused me to lose weight, (*b*) made me miserable.
        Is Antonio resigned, clear-headed, resolute, bitter, confused, sentimental, cringing, proud?
        Has his attitude to Shylock changed since I. iii? Apart from the light it throws on Shylock's character, why is the audience not shown Antonio asking for mercy?

Belmont

Lorenzo bows Portia on to the stage perhaps to a seat, although from l. 24 she should be standing. Portia and Lorenzo have been discussing the nature of friendship. Lorenzo praises Portia for her sensitive understanding of the profound claims of friendship and particularly for the way she is enduring Bassanio's absence.

2   *conceit,* understanding.

3   *god-like amity,* divine friendship. See Introduction p. 9.

SOLANIO: It is the most impenetrable cur
    That ever kept with men.

ANTONIO: Let him alone,
    I'll follow him no more with bootless prayers.   20
    He seeks my life, his reason well I know;
    I oft delivered from his forfeitures
    Many that have at times made moan to me;
    Therefore he hates me.

SOLANIO: I am sure the duke
    Will never grant this forfeiture to hold.

ANTONIO: The duke cannot deny the course of law.
    For the commodity that strangers have
    With us in Venice, if it be denied,
    Will much impeach the justice of the state,
    Since that the trade and profit of the city   30
    Consisteth of all nations. Therefore go,
    These griefs and losses have so bated me
    That I shall hardly spare a pound of flesh
    To-morrow, to my bloody creditor.
    Well gaoler, on. Pray God Bassanio come
    To see me pay his debt, and then I care not.   *[Exeunt*

SCENE FOUR

Enter PORTIA, NERISSA, LORENZO, JESSICA, *and*
BALTHAZAR

LORENZO: Madam, although I speak it in your presence,
    You have a noble and a true conceit
    Of god-like amity, which appears most strongly
    In bearing thus the absence of your lord.
    But if you knew to whom you show this honour,

7   *lover*, friend.

9   *Than . . . you*, than ordinary acts of kindness can prompt you to be.

12   *waste*, pass.

13   *do . . . love*, are linked in equally returned friendship.

15   *lineaments*, (*a*) features, limbs, (*b*) characteristics.

17   *bosom*, close.
       It was believed that very close friends bore a close likeness to each other in appearance, character, and soul. Portia refuses to be jealous of the friendship between the two men. She modestly says that as Antonio is so much akin to Bassanio the cost of rescuing him is trifling.

20   *my soul*, i.e. Bassanio, with a hint of the normal meaning. Note the underlying image, for which suggestion Portia apologizes, of the redemption of a soul, Antonio's soul, from hell.

25   *husbandry . . manage*, management and control.

28   *contemplation*, meditation on holy things.

33   *deny . . . imposition*, refuse this command imposed on you.

How true a gentleman you send relief,
How dear a lover of my lord your husband,
I know you would be prouder of the work
Than customary bounty can enforce you.

PORTIA: I never did repent for doing good,   10
Nor shall not now. For in companions
That do converse and waste the time together,
Whose souls do bear an egal yoke of love,
There must be needs a like proportion
Of lineaments, of manners, and of spirit;
Which makes me think that this Antonio,
Being the bosom lover of my lord,
Must needs be like my lord. If it be so,
How little is the cost I have bestowed
In purchasing the semblance of my soul   20
From out the state of hellish cruelty.
This comes too near the praising of myself,
Therefore no more of it; hear other things.
Lorenzo I commit into your hands
The husbandry and manage of my house,
Until my lord's return. For mine own part
I have toward heaven breathed a secret vow
To live in prayer and contemplation,
Only attended by Nerissa here,
Until her husband and my lord's return.   30
There is a monastery two miles off,
And there will we abide. I do desire you
Not to deny this imposition,
The which my love and some necessity
Now lays upon you.

LORENZO: Madam, with all my heart,
I shall obey you in all fair commands.

PORTIA: My people do already know my mind,
And will acknowledge you and Jessica

45   *Now Balthazar.* The incomplete line probably indicates a pause
      while Lorenzo and Jessica withdraw and Portia summons Bal-
      thazar forward to her.

51   *look,* look after.
52   *imagined,* (*a*) all imaginable, (*b*) (speed) of thought.
53   *traject,* ferry. Quarto and Folio have 'tranect' which some editors
      print. 'Traject', spelt 'traiect', could easily have been set up by the
      compositor erroneously as 'tranect'. 'Traject' is equivalent to
      Italian 'traghetto', ferry.
54   *trades,* plies.
56   *convenient,* due, fitting.

60   *habit,* dress.
61–2 *accomplished . . . lack.* Perhaps a reference to the opinion of some
      that women were inferior and imperfect by comparison with
      man.
63   *accoutred,* equipped.
          Any demonstration?

67   *reed voice,* harsh treble.
      mincing, dainty.

69   *quaint,* ingenious, elaborate.

142

In place of Lord Bassanio and myself.
So fare you well till we shall meet again.   40
LORENZO: Fair thoughts and happy hours attend on you.
JESSICA: I wish your ladyship all heart's content.
PORTIA: I thank you for your wish, and am well pleased
To wish it back on you. Fare you well Jessica.

> *[Exeunt Jessica and Lorenzo*

Now Balthazar.
As I have ever found thee honest-true,
So let me find thee still. Take this same letter,
And use thou all the endeavour of a man
In speed to Padua. See thou render this
Into my cousin's hand, Doctor Bellario,   50
And look what notes and garments he doth give thee,
Bring them I pray thee with imagined speed
Unto the traject, to the common ferry
Which trades to Venice. Waste no time in words
But get thee gone. I shall be there before thee.
BALTHAZAR: Madam, I go with all convenient speed.   *[Exit*
PORTIA: Come on Nerissa, I have work in hand
That you yet know not of; we'll see our husbands
Before they think of us.
NERISSA: Shall they see us?
PORTIA: They shall Nerissa; but in such a habit   60
That they shall think we are accomplished
With that we lack. I'll hold thee any wager,
When we are both accoutred like young men,
I'll prove the prettier fellow of the two,
And wear my dagger with the braver grace,
And speak between the change of man and boy
With a reed voice, and turn two mincing steps
Into a manly stride, and speak of frays
Like a fine bragging youth; and tell quaint lies
How honourable ladies sought my love,   70

72   *I ... withal,* I could not help it. With a shrug?

74   *puny,* trivial, youthful.

77   *raw,* youthful, clumsy.
      Jacks, fellows. A contemptuous word.
78   *practise,* use.
      How does Nerissa receive this—any gestures or sounds?

      This detailed description is intended to make sure the audience is clear about the disguise: Portia and Nerissa were in fact boys disguised as women disguised as boys; they would therefore appear more natural as boys. Moreover, their disguise is neither openly admitted nor openly revealed subsequently. The Elizabethan audience would enjoy the comedy and irony of the description as given by a boy.

79   *turn to,* (a) turn into, (b) embrace.
81   *lewd,* vulgar.

      Portia has taken command of the situation: she issues clear instructions, encourages others to action, and the planning of the device quickens her gay, adventurous and high spirited temperament. Her actions although obscure (Is she going to use drugs, i.e. from Doctor Bellario?) raise some hope for Antonio.

Belmont

This scene provides light relief before the trial begins; it allows for the passage of time between Portia's departure from Belmont and her appearance in court. It sets a seal of happiness on Lorenzo and Jessica, and makes very clear to the audience that she is now a Christian and assured of salvation.

1–2   *sins ... children.* Launcelot, perhaps in mock-preacher tones, reminds Jessica of the Ten Commandments.

2–3   *fear you,* fear for you. Launcelot perhaps weeps loudly or otherwise shows grief.

4   *agitation.* Perhaps 'cogitation' is meant. However, 'agitation' was used with the meaning 'consideration'.

Which I denying, they fell sick and died—
I could not do withal. Then I'll repent,
And wish for all that, that I had not killed them;
And twenty of these puny lies I'll tell,
That men shall swear I have discontinued school
Above a twelvemonth. I have within my mind
A thousand raw tricks of these bragging Jacks,
Which I will practise.
NERISSA: Why, shall we turn to men?
PORTIA: Fie, what a question's that,   80
If thou wert near a lewd interpreter.
But come, I'll tell thee all my whole device
When I am in my coach, which stays for us
At the park gate; and therefore haste away,
For we must measure twenty miles today.   [*Exeunt*

SCENE FIVE

Enter LAUNCELOT *and* JESSICA

LAUNCELOT: Yes truly; for look you, the sins of the father
are to be laid upon the children, therefore I promise ye, I fear
you. I was always plain with you, and so now I speak my
agitation of the matter. Therefore be of good cheer, for truly

5   *damned.* A further display of grief.
      Are Jessica's reactions bewildered, anxious, fearful, sprightly,
      tearful, amused, serene?

13–14 *Scylla . . . Charybdis.* In Homer's *Odyssey* Odysseus and his men
      sailed between the six-headed monster, Scylla, and the whirlpool,
      Charybdis. As the enchantress, Circe, had warned him it was
      impossible to escape, either Scylla took six men or Charybdis took
      all. Launcelot speaks with ponderous mock learning. It has been
      suggested that Launcelot pronounces Scylla so as to make a pun
      on 'Shylock'.
      your father . . . your mother. Confidential explanations.
15   *I . . . husband.* 1 *Corinthians*, vii. 14, 'the unbelieving wife is
      sanctified by the husband.' In what mood should Jessica say this?
17–21 *Truly . . . money.* Launcelot relapses into a familiar style of speak-
      ing.

25   *corners,* quiet corners.

27   *are out,* have fallen out.

31   *best . . . wit,* most elegant conversation.
32–3 *discourse . . . parrots,* i.e. the only praiseworthy conversation will
      be that of parrots that repeat the same phrase.
34   *stomachs,* appetites.
35   *wit-snapper,* one who seizes every chance to quibble.

I think you are damned. There is but one hope in it that can do you any good, and that is but a kind of bastard hope neither.

JESSICA: And what hope is that I pray thee?

LAUNCELOT: Marry you may partly hope that your father got you not, that you are not the Jew's daughter.

JESSICA: That were a kind of bastard hope indeed, so the sins of my mother should be visited upon me.   11

LAUNCELOT: Truly then I fear you are damned both by father and mother. Thus when I shun Scylla your father, I fall into Charybdis your mother; well, you are gone both ways.

JESSICA: I shall be saved by my husband, he hath made me a Christian.

LAUNCELOT: Truly the more to blame he, we were Christians enow before, e'en as many as could well live one by another. This making of Christians will raise the price of hogs: if we grow all to be pork-eaters, we shall not shortly have a rasher on the coals for money.   21

Enter LORENZO

JESSICA: I'll tell my husband, Launcelot, what you say. Here he comes.   23

LORENZO: I shall grow jealous of you shortly Launcelot, if you thus get my wife into corners.

JESSICA: Nay, you need not fear us Lorenzo. Launcelot and I are out. He tells me flatly there is no mercy for me in heaven, because I am a Jew's daughter. And he says you are no good member of the commonwealth, for in converting Jews to Christians, you raise the price of pork.

LORENZO: I think the best grace of wit will shortly turn into silence, and discourse grow commendable in none only but parrots. Go in sirrah, bid them prepare for dinner.

LAUNCELOT: That is done sir, they have all stomachs.

LORENZO: Goodly Lord, what a wit-snapper are you. Then bid them prepare dinner.

37   *only . . . word,* to lay the table is the only thing left to do.
38   *cover,* (*a*) lay the table, (*b*) put one's hat on.
39   *Not . . . duty,* i.e. I will not be so impolite as to put on my hat
      while speaking to you.
40   *Yet . . . occasion,* disputing at every opportunity.

45   *table,* i.e. food.
46   *covered,* i.e. the meat will have covers on it.
47   *humours . . . conceits,* moods and fancy shall decide.
48   *O . . . discretion,* what precious distinctions he makes! To whom is
      this part of the speech addressed?
      suited, made to match.
49   *planted,* stationed.
50   *army . . . words.* In defiance of the proverb, 'Few words are good
      words'. 'army' should be emphasized.
51   *stand . . . place,* have a better position.
52   *Garnished,* (*a*) clothed in motley, (*b*) provided with a similar
      vocabulary.
      tricksy word, (*a*) fine phrase, (*b*) a word whose meaning can be
      twisted.
53   *Defy . . . matter,* make nonsense of the meaning.
      how . . . Jessica. During this conversation is Jessica—listening,
      moping, dejected, doing something else, laughing, thoughtful?
56–61 The joys of heaven are a reward for a good life and a compensa-
      tion for an unhappy one. Bassanio cannot claim the compensation
      so he must earn the reward (Arden).
60   *merit it.* Some editors prefer 'mean it, then'. The Quarto and
      Folio reading is 'meane it, it'.
62   *play . . . match,* make a bet.
63   *lay,* stake.
65   *Pawned,* staked.
      rude, barbarous, rough-mannered.
      A quick change from grave sincerity to happy, teasing cross-
      chat.

LAUNCELOT: That is done too sir, only 'cover' is the word.   37

LORENZO: Will you cover then sir?

LAUNCELOT: Not so sir neither, I know my duty.

LORENZO: Yet more quarrelling with occasion. Wilt thou show
  the whole wealth of thy wit in an instant? I pray thee understand a plain man in his plain meaning. Go to thy fellows, bid
  them cover the table, serve in the meat, and we will come in to
  dinner.

LAUNCELOT: For the table sir, it shall be served in, for the meat
  sir, it shall be covered, for your coming in to dinner sir, why
  let it be as humours and conceits shall govern.   [*Exit*

LORENZO: O dear discretion, how his words are suited.   48
  The fool hath planted in his memory
  An army of good words, and I do know
  A many fools that stand in better place,
  Garnished like him, that for a tricksy word
  Defy the matter. How cheer'st thou Jessica?   53
  And now good sweet, say thy opinion,
  How dost thou like the Lord Bassanio's wife?

JESSICA: Past all expressing. It is very meet
  The Lord Bassanio live an upright life,
  For having such a blessing in his lady,
  He finds the joys of heaven here on earth,
  And if on earth he do not merit it,
  In reason he should never come to heaven.
  Why, if two gods should play some heavenly match,   62
  And on the wager lay two earthly women,
  And Portia one, there must be something else
  Pawned with the other, for the poor rude world
  Hath not her fellow.

LORENZO: Even such a husband
  Hast thou of me, as she is for a wife.

JESSICA: Nay, but ask my opinion too of that.

LORENZO: I will anon, first let us go to dinner.

70   *stomach*, (*a*) inclination, (*b*) appetite.
71   *table-talk*, (*a*) talk about food, (*b*) conversation at table.

73   *digest*, (*a*) absorb food, (*b*) put it in place.
       set . . . forth, (*a*) praise, (*b*) prepare for a feast.
        What kind of exit would be appropriate?

JESSICA: Nay, let me praise you while I have a stomach.   70
LORENZO: No pray thee, let it serve for table-talk,
     Then howsoe'er thou speak'st, 'mong other things
     I shall digest it.
JESSICA: Well, I'll set you forth.   [*Exeunt*

Venice

The entry should be a formal, ceremonial procession presenting the pageantry of the city nobility. Does the Duke enter first or last? The positioning of the principal characters needs careful thought. What persons other than those mentioned would you expect in a court of law? What stage properties are required?

2   Antonio steps forward and bows.

3   *answer*, i.e. answer the charge brought by.

6   *dram*, jot, grain.

7   *qualify*, soften, moderate.

13   *tyranny*, violence.

16   *Make room*. Shylock's entry is important. Does he come alone or accompanied, arrogant and scornful or furtive and suspicious? Do the spectators recoil from him, murmur at him, jeer and curse him, or receive him in stony silence?

18   *leadest . . . fashion*, prolong this show.

20   *remorse*, pity.

21   *strange apparent*, strange-seeming.

22   *where*, whereas. *exacts*. An old form of the second person.

ACT FOUR

SCENE ONE

Enter the DUKE, *the Magnificoes,* ANTONIO, BASSANIO, GRATIANO, SOLANIO, *and others*

DUKE: What, is Antonio here?

ANTONIO: Ready, so please your grace.

DUKE: I am sorry for thee, thou art come to answer
    A stony adversary, an inhuman wretch,
    Uncapable of pity, void and empty
    From any dram of mercy.

ANTONIO: I have heard
    Your grace hath ta'en great pains to qualify
    His rigorous course; but since he stands obdurate,
    And that no lawful means can carry me
    Out of his envy's reach, I do oppose   10
    My patience to his fury, and am armed
    To suffer with a quietness of spirit,
    The very tyranny and rage of his.

DUKE: Go one and call the Jew into the court.

SOLANIO: He is ready at the door, he comes my lord.

Enter SHYLOCK

DUKE: Make room, and let him stand before our face.
    Shylock, the world thinks, and I think so too,
    That thou but leadest this fashion of thy malice
    To the last hour of act, and then 'tis thought
    Thou'lt show thy mercy and remorse more strange   20
    Than is thy strange apparent cruelty;
    And where thou now exacts the penalty,
    Which is a pound of this poor merchant's flesh,

24   *loose*, give up, release.

26   *moiety*, portion.

32   Turks and Tartars were notorious for their savage cruelty and inhumanity.

33   *offices*, duties.

34   *gentle*, gentlemanly, courteous.
       Should Shylock react by movement or gesture or remain unmoved during this speech?

35   *possessed*, told, informed.
       See Introduction p. 20 for this speech.

36–7 *And . . . bond*. Any gesture?

38   *danger*, harm, injury.

41   *carrion*, dead.
       Salerio had asked a similar question III. i, 42.

42–3 *I'll . . . humour*. The question is not, of course, to the point, but Shylock contemptuously galls the onlookers.

43   *humour*, fancy, whim.

46   *baned*, poisoned.

47   *gaping pig*, i.e. a pig's head served at table.

50   *affection*, natural liking.

51   *passion*, feeling, emotion.

56   *woollen*, covered with a woollen cloth.

Thou wilt not only loose the forfeiture,
But touched with human gentleness and love,
Forgive a moiety of the principal,
Glancing an eye of pity on his losses
That have of late so huddled on his back,
Enow to press a royal merchant down,
And pluck commiseration of his state   30
From brassy bosoms and rough hearts of flint,
From stubborn Turks, and Tartars never trained
To offices of tender courtesy.
We all expect a gentle answer Jew.

SHYLOCK: I have possessed your grace of what I purpose;
And by our holy Sabbath have I sworn
To have the due and forfeit of my bond.
If you deny it, let the danger light
Upon your charter and your city's freedom.
You'll ask me why I rather choose to have   40
A weight of carrion flesh, than to receive
Three thousand ducats. I'll not answer that,
But say it is my humour; is it answered?
What if my house be troubled with a rat,
And I be pleased to give ten thousand ducats
To have it baned? What, are you answered yet?
Some men there are love not a gaping pig;
Some that are mad if they behold a cat;
And others when the bagpipe sings i' the nose,
Cannot contain their urine; for affection,   50
Mistress of passion, sways it to the mood
Of what it likes or loathes. Now for your answer:
As there is no firm reason to be rendered
Why he cannot abide a gaping pig;
Why he, a harmless necessary cat;
Why he, a woollen bagpipe; but of force
Must yield to such inevitable shame,

58 *As . . . offended,* to give offence to other people because he himself was offended first.

Shylock's illustrations, which by implication put Antonio in the same class as pigs, cats and bagpipes, are deliberately offensive. Has his treatment at the hands of Christians given him justification? (I. iii, 100–125).

60 *lodged,* fixed.

Shylock, secure in his stand, crowns his remarks with an open admission of his hatred. How do the spectators receive this?

62 *losing suit,* i.e. Shylock will lose three thousand ducats if he wins his case.

How do the onlookers react to Shylock's speech?

70 *think,* bear in mind that.

72 *main flood,* high tide.
bate, lower.

76 *and to make,* and bid them to make.
77 *fretten,* tossed to and fro.

81 *moe,* more.
means, pleas, attempts.
82 *But . . . conveniency,* but as quickly and as simply as is fitting. Antonio is suffering under the prolonged tension; he begs for the sentence to be passed as he sees no way of escape.

87 *draw,* take.
88 *How . . . none. James,* ii. 13; *St. Matthew,* v. 7.
89 For this speech see Introduction p. 20.

As to offend himself being offended;
So can I give no reason, nor I will not,
More than a lodged hate and a certain loathing   60
I bear Antonio, that I follow thus
A losing suit against him. Are you answered?
ASSANIO: This is no answer thou unfeeling man,
  To excuse the current of thy cruelty.
HYLOCK: I am not bound to please thee with my answer.
ASSANIO: Do all men kill the things they do not love?
HYLOCK: Hates any man the thing he would not kill?
ASSANIO: Every offence is not a hate at first.
HYLOCK: What, wouldst thou have a serpent sting thee twice?
ANTONIO: I pray you think you question with the Jew.   70
  You may as well go stand upon the beach
  And bid the main flood bate his usual height;
  You may as well use question with the wolf
  Why he hath made the ewe bleat for the lamb;
  You may as well forbid the mountain pines
  To wag their high tops and to make no noise
  When they are fretten with the gusts of heaven;
  You may as well do any thing most hard
  As seek to soften that—than which what's harder?
  His Jewish heart. Therefore I do beseech you   80
  Make no moe offers, use no farther means,
  But with all brief and plain conveniency
  Let me have judgement, and the Jew his will.
ASSANIO: For thy three thousand ducats here is six.
HYLOCK: If every ducat in six thousand ducats
  Were in six parts, and every part a ducat,
  I would not draw them, I would have my bond.
DUKE: How shalt thou hope for mercy, rendering none?
HYLOCK: What judgement shall I dread, doing no wrong?
  You have among you many a purchased slave,   90
  Which like your asses, and your dogs and mules,

92   *abject,* wretched.
        parts, work, tasks.

97   *seasoned . . . viands,* gain a taste for such delicacies as you eat.
        How is Shylock's challenge received? Is it a plea for the down-trodden slaves or a debating point?

103   *I . . . judgement.* This is the climax of Shylock's claim at this stage it is spoken with tremendous force. It is an interesting contrast with Portia's 'I stand for sacrifice' just before her arrival.
       answer. Hitherto Shylock has been asked for answers, now he demands the fatal answer from his questioners.

104   *Upon,* by.

111– An extravagant promise but spoken sincerely. It shows for a
13   moment as it were the vital point which saved Antonio—'one drop of blood'.

114   *tainted,* sinful, sick.

115   *Meetest,* fittest.
        Is Antonio's mood self-pitying, unctuous, histrionic, dignified, sentimental, that of a poseur, of pious resignation of a scapegoat, or a willing sacrifice?

121–6 Note the linking of thought: 'whet', 'knife', 'cut', 'keen', 'axe', 'sharp'. 'pierce'.

You use in abject and in slavish parts,
Because you bought them, shall I say to you,
Let them be free, marry them to your heirs?
Why sweat they under burthens? Let their beds
Be made as soft as yours, and let their palates
Be seasoned with such viands. You will answer,
'The slaves are ours'; so do I answer you.
The pound of flesh which I demand of him
Is dearly bought, 'tis mine and I will have it.   100
If you deny me, fie upon your law,
There is no force in the decrees of Venice.
I stand for judgement—answer, shall I have it?

DUKE: Upon my power I may dismiss this court,
Unless Bellario a learned doctor,
Whom I have sent for to determine this,
Come here today.

SOLANIO: My lord, here stays without
A messenger with letters from the doctor,
New come from Padua.

DUKE: Bring us the letters. Call the messenger.   110

BASSANIO: Good cheer Antonio. What man, courage yet.
The Jew shall have my flesh, blood, bones, and all,
Ere thou shalt lose for me one drop of blood.

ANTONIO: I am a tainted wether of the flock,
Meetest for death. The weakest kind of fruit
Drops earliest to the ground, and so let me.
You cannot better be employed Bassanio,
Than to live still and write mine epitaph.

             Enter NERISSA, *dressed like a lawyer's clerk*

DUKE: Came you from Padua from Bellario?

NERISSA: From both, my lord. Bellario greets your grace.   120
                                        [*Presents a letter*

BASSANIO: Why dost thou whet thy knife so earnestly?

123   *sole . . . soul.* What feeling is expressed by this pun—mirth, anguish, bitterness, fear, anger?

128   *inexecrable,* too vile for cursing, or, unable to be execrated adequately (Sisson).

129   Let justice take away your life even if justice itself is thereby guilty of the crime.

131   *Pythagoras.* A Greek philosopher who taught that the souls of men passed after death into animals, and that the souls of animals passed into certain men and determined their characters.

132   *infuse,* pour in, insinuate. It was held that the divine soul was 'infused' into the body at birth.

134   *wolf . . . slaughter.* A possible reference to the execution of Roderigo Lopez, the Queen's physician, on 7 June 1594.

135   *fell,* fierce.

138   *starved,* fiercely greedy.
       Gratiano's nerves are frayed almost to breaking so that he raves at Shylock.

139–   Shylock dismisses such lightweights as Bassanio with patronizing
42   contempt.

139   *rail,* argue.

140   *offendest,* injurest.

144   *doctor,* i.e. of law.

150   There is no indication in the Quarto or Folio that a clerk should read the letter.

SHYLOCK: To cut the forfeiture from that bankrupt there.
GRATIANO: Not on thy sole, but on thy soul harsh Jew,
  Thou mak'st thy knife keen. But no metal can,
  No, not the hangman's axe, bear half the keenness
  Of thy sharp envy. Can no prayers pierce thee?
SHYLOCK: No, none that thou hast wit enough to make.
GRATIANO: O, be thou damned, inexecrable dog,
  And for thy life let justice be accused.
  Thou almost mak'st me waver in my faith,   130
  To hold opinion with Pythagoras,
  That souls of animals infuse themselves
  Into the trunks of men. Thy currish spirit
  Governed a wolf, who hanged for human slaughter,
  Even from the gallows did his fell soul fleet,
  And whilst thou layest in thy unhallowed dam,
  Infused itself in thee; for thy desires
  Are wolvish, bloody, starved, and ravenous.
SHYLOCK: Till thou canst rail the seal from off my bond,
  Thou but offendest thy lungs to speak so loud.   140
  Repair thy wit good youth, or it will fall
  To cureless ruin. I stand here for law.
DUKE: This letter from Bellario doth commend
  A young and learned doctor to our court.
  Where is he?
NERISSA: He attendeth here hard by
  To know your answer whether you'll admit him.
DUKE: With all my heart. Some three or four of you
  Go give him courteous conduct to this place.
  Meantime the court shall hear Bellario's letter.   149
CLERK: [Reads] 'Your grace shall understand that at the receipt
  of your letter I am very sick, but in the instant that your
  messenger came, in loving visitation was with me a young
  doctor of Rome; his name is Balthazar. I acquainted him with
  the cause in controversy between the Jew and Antonio the

158   *fill up*, fulfil.

159– *no . . . estimation*, no obstacle to prevent his receiving respect and
60   esteem.

162   *trial*, endeavour (in the case).

165   Do the spectators express any feelings at Portia's appearance?
       Give . . . hand. Portia bows over the Duke's hand.

166   *take . . . place*, i.e. in the judge's chair.
167   *difference*, dispute.
168   *That . . . court*, which causes the present case to be brought before
       the court.
169   *throughly*, thoroughly.

172   Is Shylock contemptuous or cautious?
173   *suit*, law suit.
       follow, are engaged in.
174   *rule*, order, i.e. so correctly ordered.
175   *impugn . . . proceed*, find fault with your presentation of the case.
176   *danger*, power.

178   *Then . . . merciful*, i.e. the Jew will, *of course*, be merciful, or, the
       only way out is for the Jew to be merciful.
179   Is Shylock aggressive, indifferent, amused, mocking, curious?
180   *The . . . strained*, mercy is a virtue that cannot be compelled.
181–2 *It . . . beneath. Ecclesiasticus*, xxxv. 20. Mercy is seasonable in time
       of affliction, as clouds of rain in the time of drought.

merchant; we turned o'er many books together; he is furnished
with my opinion, which bettered with his own learning, the
greatness whereof I cannot enough commend, comes with him
at my importunity, to fill up your grace's request in my stead.
I beseech you let his lack of years be no impediment to let him
lack a reverend estimation, for I never knew so young a body
with so old a head. I leave him to your gracious acceptance,
whose trial shall better publish his commendation.'

DUKE: You hear the learned Bellario what he writes,
And here, I take it, is the doctor come.

Enter PORTIA, *dressed like a doctor of laws*

Give me your hand. Come you from old Bellario?
PORTIA: I did my lord.
DUKE: You are welcome, take your place.
Are you acquainted with the difference
That holds this present question in the court?
PORTIA: I am informed throughly of the cause.
Which is the merchant here? And which the Jew?   170
DUKE: Antonio and old Shylock, both stand forth.
PORTIA: Is your name Shylock?
SHYLOCK: Shylock is my name.
PORTIA: Of a strange nature is the suit you follow,
Yet in such rule that the Venetian law
Cannot impugn you as you do proceed.
You stand within his danger, do you not?
ANTONIO: Ay, so he says.
PORTIA: Do you confess the bond?
ANTONIO: I do.
PORTIA: Then must the Jew be merciful.
SHYLOCK: On what compulsion must I? Tell me that.
PORTIA: The quality of mercy is not strained,   180
It droppeth as the gentle rain from heaven
Upon the place beneath. It is twice blest,

185   *crown*, kingly authority.

186   *shows*, stands for, is the sign of.

187   *attribute*, symbol, quality.

192–3 *And . . . justice*. Almost proverbial.

193   *seasons*, moderates, tempers. i.e. If in the Day of Judgement justice only were to be given, not one of us would be righteous enough to obtain salvation.

196   *We . . . mercy*, i.e. the Lord's Prayer.

198   *deeds of mercy*. Traditionally they were seven in number, based on *St. Matthew*, xxv. 34–46.
       Do the onlookers respond to this speech and to Shylock's reply?

199   *mitigate*, temper (with mercy).
       Galatians, iii–iv treats of the letter of the law and of love fulfilling the law in a similar way. See also *Romans*, xiii.

202   *My . . . head*. The cry of the Jews condemning Christ has been suggested as a parallel: 'His blood be on us, and on our children' *St. Matthew*, xxvii. 25.
       deeds, echoes l. 198. Shylock cries out with great force. The words are a challenge to fate, to an Elizabethan a deadly sin, and they are the turning point of the scene.

204   *discharge*, pay.

207–8 Bassanio offers to enter into a bond with a similar forfeit on behalf of Antonio.

210   *malice . . . truth*, hatred is overthrowing uprightness. Shylock's insistence on the law is not because his principles are high but because he hates Antonio. Bassanio pleads that as Shylock is using the law for an evil purpose, Portia would be justified in setting aside the law.

It blesseth him that gives, and him that takes.
'Tis mightiest in the mightiest, it becomes
The thronèd monarch better than his crown.
His sceptre shows the force of temporal power,
The attribute to awe and majesty,
Wherein doth sit the dread and fear of kings.
But mercy is above this sceptred sway,
It is enthroned in the hearts of kings,   190
It is an attribute to God himself;
And earthly power doth then show likest God's
When mercy seasons justice. Therefore Jew,
Though justice be thy plea, consider this,
That in the course of justice, none of us
Should see salvation. We do pray for mercy,
And that same prayer doth teach us all to render
The deeds of mercy. I have spoke thus much
To mitigate the justice of thy plea,
Which if thou follow, this strict court of Venice   200
Must needs give sentence 'gainst the merchant there.
SHYLOCK: My deeds upon my head, I crave the law,
  The penalty and forfeit of my bond.
PORTIA: Is he not able to discharge the money?
BASSANIO: Yes, here I tender it for him in the court,
  Yea, twice the sum, if that will not suffice,
  I will be bound to pay it ten times o'er
  On forfeit of my hands, my head, my heart.
  If this will not suffice, it must appear
  That malice bears down truth. And I beseech you   210
  Wrest once the law to your authority:
  To do a great right, do a little wrong,
  And curb this cruel devil of his will.
PORTIA: It must not be, there is no power in Venice
  Can alter a decree established.

216   *precedent.* The interpretation of the laws is guided by judgements given in previous cases.

217   *error,* injustice.

219   *Daniel.* A reference to the *History of Susanna* in the *Apocrypha.* Daniel, the wise young judge, was a 'young youth' to whom God had given the 'honour of an elder'. By his skilful cross-examination he proved the guilt of the two corrupt elders out of their own mouths. Portia's youthful appearance makes the comparison an apt one. The wisdom of Daniel was proverbial.

222   *Here . . . is.* Shylock offers it with eager haste.

225   *perjury.* Shylock draws the line at perjury but not at judicial murder!

229   *Nearest . . . heart.* Apparently specified in the bond (See I. iii, 147)

231   *tenour,* terms of the bond.

244   *Hath . . . to,* fully allows and enforces (Arden).

247   *more elder.* Emphatic double comparative.

'Twill be recorded for a precedent,
And many an error by the same example
Will rush into the state. It cannot be.

SHYLOCK: A Daniel come to judgement. Yea a Daniel.
O wise young judge how I do honour thee.   220

PORTIA: I pray you let me look upon the bond.

SHYLOCK: Here 'tis most reverend doctor, here it is.

PORTIA: Shylock there's thrice thy money offered thee.

SHYLOCK: An oath, an oath, I have an oath in heaven.
Shall I lay perjury upon my soul?
No, not for Venice.

PORTIA: Why this bond is forfeit,
And lawfully by this the Jew may claim
A pound of flesh, to be by him cut off
Nearest the merchant's heart. Be merciful,
Take thrice thy money, bid me tear the bond.   230

SHYLOCK: When it is paid according to the tenour.
It doth appear you are a worthy judge;
You know the law, your exposition
Hath been most sound. I charge you by the law,
Whereof you are a well-deserving pillar,
Proceed to judgement. By my soul I swear
There is no power in the tongue of man
To alter me, I stay here on my bond.

ANTONIO: Most heartily I do beseech the court
To give the judgement.

PORTIA: Why then thus it is: 240
You must prepare your bosom for his knife.

SHYLOCK: O noble judge, o excellent young man.

PORTIA: For the intent and purpose of the law
Hath full relation to the penalty,
Which here appeareth due upon the bond.

SHYLOCK: 'Tis very true. O wise and upright judge,
How much more elder art thou than thy looks.

249ff. This prolonged arguing over the letter of the bond while it is almost unbearably harrowing also remorselessly condemns Shylock, and (as Granville Barker noted) it strips Shylock's dignity from him.

253   *charge,* expense.

260   *armed.* Possibly a glance at *Ephesians,* vi. 11–18.

263   *Fortune.* She was regarded as a goddess whose favours were granted in a random manner.

264   *still,* always.
       use, practice, custom.

270   *process,* (*a*) course of events, (*b*) legal action.

272   *bid . . . judge.* Dramatic irony.

277   *with . . . heart.* Quibbles by men about to die occur elsewhere in Shakespeare's plays, they show a last flicker of courage, a tilt at fate.

278–   Bassanio offers to sacrifice all for his friend; it is the supreme
83   offer of friendship.

PORTIA: Therefore lay bare your bosom.

SHYLOCK: Ay, his breast,
  So says the bond, doth it not noble judge?
  'Nearest his heart', those are the very words.   250

PORTIA: It is so. Are there balance here to weigh
  The flesh?

SHYLOCK: I have them ready.

PORTIA: Have by some surgeon Shylock, on your charge,
  To stop his wounds, lest he do bleed to death.

SHYLOCK: Is it so nominated in the bond?

PORTIA: It is not so expressed, but what of that?
  'Twere good you do so much for charity.

SHYLOCK: I cannot find it, 'tis not in the bond.

PORTIA: You merchant, have you any thing to say?

ANTONIO: But little; I am armed and well prepared   260
  Give me your hand Bassanio, fare you well.
  Grieve not that I am fallen to this for you,
  For herein Fortune shows herself more kind
  Than is her custom: it is still her use
  To let the wretched man outlive his wealth,
  To view with hollow eye and wrinkled brow
  An age of poverty; from which lingering penance
  Of such misery doth she cut me off.
  Commend me to your honourable wife.
  Tell her the process of Antonio's end.   270
  Say how I loved you, speak me fair in death;
  And when the tale is told, bid her be judge
  Whether Bassanio had not once a love.
  Repent but you that you shall lose your friend,
  And he repents not that he pays your debt.
  For if the Jew do cut but deep enough,
  I'll pay it presently with all my heart.

BASSANIO: Antonio, I am married to a wife
  Which is as dear to me as life itself,

284–5 A flicker of humour plays through the dramatic irony.

286–8 Gratiano, irrepressibly offers only his wife and Nerissa's tone in replying may suggest that she is ruffled.
    Dramatically these exchanges remind the audience of some device to come, the momentary loosening of tension and suspense makes Portia's pronouncement of sentence a greater shock.

292 *Barrabas*. The robber whom Pilate released at the demand of the Jewish mob.

295–6 Portia pronounces sentence with formal emphasis. How do the

298–9 spectators receive it? It has been suggested that Shylock receives the sentence with triumph raising aloft the scales and his dagger in a kind of parody of the sword and scales of Justice.

300 *Come prepare*. He turns to Antonio. How should this be spoken— thickly with emotion, exalted as a priest about to offer a sacrifice, with a triumphant shout, with quiet, sadistic enjoyment?

301 *Tarry a little*. Portia's manner is urbane and courteous in the first three lines, she does not cry, 'Hold!' Is she examining the bond as she speaks?

304–8 *Take then . . . Venice*. Spoken emphatically.

309 *O . . . judge*. An electrifying shout—or screech. Do the spectators reveal their feelings?

310 *Thyself . . . act*. Any stage business?

But life itself, my wife, and all the world,   280
Are not with me esteemed above thy life.
I would lose all, ay sacrifice them all
Here to this devil, to deliver you.

PORTIA: Your wife would give you little thanks for that,
If she were by to hear you make the offer.

GRATIANO: I have a wife whom I protest I love,
I would she were in heaven, so she could
Entreat some power to change this currish Jew.

NERISSA: 'Tis well you offer it behind her back,
The wish would make else an unquiet house.   290

SHYLOCK: [*Aside*] These be the Christian husbands. I have a
daughter—
Would any of the stock of Barrabas
Had been her husband rather than a Christian.
[*Aloud*] We trifle time, I pray thee pursue sentence.

PORTIA: A pound of that same merchant's flesh is thine;
The court awards it, and the law doth give it.

SHYLOCK: Most rightful judge.

PORTIA: And you must cut this flesh from off his breast;
The law allows it, and the court awards it.

SHYLOCK: Most learned judge. A sentence. Come prepare.   300

PORTIA: Tarry a little, there is something else.
This bond doth give thee here no jot of blood,
The words expressly are 'a pound of flesh'.
Take then thy bond, take thou thy pound of flesh,
But in the cutting it, if thou dost shed
One drop of Christian blood, thy lands and goods
Are by the laws of Venice confiscate
Unto the state of Venice.

GRATIANO: O upright judge—mark, Jew—O learned judge.

SHYLOCK: Is that the law?

PORTIA: Thyself shalt see the act.   310
For as thou urgest justice, be assured

316   *soft,* not so fast.
317   *all,* nothing but.

324–6 *in . . . scruple,* by a twentieth of a scruple, or, by a fraction of that
       twentieth.

327   *estimation,* weight, amount.

329   *Daniel.* Gratiano seizes on the point that Daniel had convicted the
       elders out of their own evidence.
330   *on the hip.* An ironical echo of Shylock's wish, I. iii, 40.

342   *question,* legal argument.

Thou shalt have justice more than thou desirest.

GRATIANO: O learned judge—mark, Jew—a learned judge.

SHYLOCK: I take this offer then; pay the bond thrice
And let the Christian go.

BASSANIO: Here is the money.

PORTIA: Soft,
The Jew shall have all justice—soft no haste—
He shall have nothing but the penalty.

GRATIANO: O Jew, an upright judge, a learned judge.

PORTIA: Therefore prepare thee to cut off the flesh.   320
Shed thou no blood, nor cut thou less nor more
But just a pound of flesh. If thou tak'st more
Or less than a just pound, be it but so much
As makes it light or heavy in the substance,
Of the division of the twentieth part
Of one poor scruple, nay if the scale do turn
But in the estimation of a hair,
Thou diest, and all thy goods are confiscate.

GRATIANO: A second Daniel, a Daniel, Jew.
Now infidel I have you on the hip.   330

PORTIA: Why doth the Jew pause? Take thy forfeiture.

SHYLOCK: Give me my principal, and let me go.

BASSANIO: I have it ready for thee, here it is.

PORTIA: He hath refused it in the open court.
He shall have merely justice and his bond.

GRATIANO: A Daniel still say I, a second Daniel.
I thank thee Jew for teaching me that word.

SHYLOCK: Shall I not have barely my principal?

PORTIA: Thou shalt have nothing but the forfeiture
To be so taken at thy peril Jew.   340

SHYLOCK: Why then the devil give him good of it.
I'll stay no longer question.

PORTIA: Tarry Jew,
The law hath yet another hold on you.

345– *If . . . voice.* Does Portia quote this from memory or does Nerissa
52   hand her a statute book?

348   *contrive*, plot.
349   *seize*, lawfully take possession of.

352   *'gainst . . . voice*, in spite of any contrary opinion or vote.
353   *predicament*, category, class.

358   *rehearsed*, stated.
359   How does Shylock kneel—stubbornly, sullenly, hurriedly,
      fawningly, bitterly?
360   *leave . . . thyself*, i.e. Judas-like.

368   *humbleness . . . fine*, a humble request for mercy may persuade us
      to reduce the punishment to a fine.
369   *Ay . . . Antonio*, i.e. Antonio's half is not to be reduced to a fine.

372–4 *you . . . live.* Perhaps a glance at *Ecclesiasticus*, xxxiv. 22, 'He that
      taketh away his neighbour's living, slayeth him'. An echo too
      of Marlowe's *Jew of Malta*, II. i, 147ff.

375   Does Gratiano's fierce jeering commentary show a better or
      worse attitude than Shylock's?

It is enacted in the laws of Venice,
If it be proved against an alien
That by direct, or indirect attempts
He seek the life of any citizen,
The party 'gainst the which he doth contrive
Shall seize one half his goods, the other half
Comes to the privy coffer of the state,   350
And the offender's life lies in the mercy
Of the duke only, 'gainst all other voice.
In which predicament I say thou stand'st;
For it appears by manifest proceeding,
That indirectly, and directly too,
Thou hast contrived against the very life
Of the defendant; and thou hast incurred
The danger formerly by me rehearsed.
Down therefore, and beg mercy of the duke.
GRATIANO. Beg that thou mayst have leave to hang thyself. 360
And yet thy wealth being forfeit to the state,
Thou hast not left the value of a cord,
Therefore thou must be hanged at the state's charge.
DUKE: That thou shalt see the difference of our spirit,
I pardon thee thy life before thou ask it.
For half thy wealth, it is Antonio's,
The other half comes to the general state,
Which humbleness may drive unto a fine.
PORTIA: Ay, for the state, not for Antonio.
SHYLOCK: Nay, take my life and all, pardon not that.   370
You take my house, when you do take the prop
That doth sustain my house; you take my life,
When you do take the means whereby I live.
PORTIA: What mercy can you render him Antonio?
GRATIANO: A halter gratis, nothing else for God's sake.
ANTONIO: So please my lord the duke and all the court

377–   *To . . . daughter,* i.e. Shylock will keep half his wealth withou
  81   paying the proposed fine, the other half Antonio will keep in
    trust for Lorenzo. See Introduction, p. 10.

377   *quit,* remit.

379   *in use,* in trust.

383   *Christian,* i.e. Antonio attempts to save Shylock's soul. How
    should Shylock receive this—joyfully, calmly, with abhorrence
    How do the spectators receive it?

384   *record a gift,* sign a statement making a gift.

390   *I am content.* How should this be said—quickly, angrily, resent
    fully, sneeringly, in anguish, humbly? (See l. 392).

395   *ten more,* i.e. a jury of twelve. A grim current joke was to call the
    jurymen 'godfathers'.

397   Any stage business from the spectators as Shylock leaves
    Should he leave in a frozen silence or in derision?

398   *desire . . . pardon,* ask pardon of your Grace.

402   *gratify,* reward.

403   *bound,* indebted. An echo of the other 'bond'.

To quit the fine for one half of his goods,
I am content—so he will let me have
The other half in use—to render it
Upon his death unto the gentleman   380
That lately stole his daughter.
Two things provided more, that for this favour,
He presently become a Christian;
The other, that he do record a gift
Here in the court of all he dies possessed
Unto his son Lorenzo and his daughter.
DUKE: He shall do this, or else I do recant
The pardon that I late pronounced here.
PORTIA: Art thou contented Jew? What dost thou say?
SHYLOCK: I am content.
PORTIA: Clerk, draw a deed of gift.   390
SHYLOCK: I pray you give me leave to go from hence,
I am not well. Send the deed after me,
And I will sign it.
DUKE: Get thee gone, but do it.
GRATIANO: In christening shalt thou have two godfathers;
Had I been judge, thou shouldst have had ten more,
To bring thee to the gallows, not to the font.

                        [*Exit Shylock*

DUKE: Sir I entreat you home with me to dinner.
PORTIA: I humbly do desire your grace of pardon,
I must away this night toward Padua,
And it is meet I presently set forth.   400
DUKE: I am sorry that your leisure serves you not.
Antonio, gratify this gentleman,
For in my mind you are much bound to him.

              [*Exeunt Duke and his train*

BASSANIO: Most worthy gentleman, I and my friend
Have by your wisdom been this day acquitted
Of grievous penalties, in lieu whereof

408   *cope*, recompense, offer as an equivalent for.

415   *know me*, (*a*) recognize me, (*b*) let this be an introduction. A light
       touch of dramatic irony.

417   *of . . . further*, i.e. I feel compelled to try further to persuade you.

420   *pardon me*, i.e. for his insistence.

422   *gloves*. These gloves may be Antonio's (see ll. 402–3), and Portia
       may then turn to Bassanio. Alternatively, both lines may refer to
       Bassanio whose ring is revealed when he takes off his gloves.

423,   *for your love, you in love*, out of courtesy or friendship. Portia
425   impishly embarrasses Bassanio.

436   *how . . . answered*. Proverbially beggars cannot be choosers.

440   *'scuse*, excuse.

Three thousand ducats due unto the Jew,
We freely cope your courteous pains withal.

ANTONIO: And stand indebted over and above
　　In love and service to you evermore.　　　　　　　　410

PORTIA: He is well paid that is well satisfied,
　　And I, delivering you, am satisfied
　　And therein do account myself well paid.
　　My mind was never yet more mercenary.
　　I pray you, know me when we meet again.
　　I wish you well, and so I take my leave.

BASSANIO: Dear sir, of force I must attempt you further:
　　Take some remembrance of us as a tribute,
　　Not as a fee. Grant me two things I pray you,
　　Not to deny me, and to pardon me.　　　　　　　　420

PORTIA: You press me far, and therefore I will yield.
　　[*To Antonio*] Give me your gloves, I'll wear them for your sake.
　　[*To Bassanio*] And for your love I'll take this ring from you.
　　Do not draw back your hand, I'll take no more,
　　And you in love shall not deny me this.

BASSANIO: This ring good sir, alas it is a trifle,
　　I will not shame myself to give you this.

PORTIA: I will have nothing else but only this,
　　And now methinks I have a mind to it.

BASSANIO: There's more depends on this than on the value. 430
　　The dearest ring in Venice will I give you,
　　And find it out by proclamation.
　　Only for this, I pray you, pardon me.

PORTIA: I see sir, you are liberal in offers.
　　You taught me first to beg, and now methinks
　　You teach me how a beggar should be answered.

BASSANIO: Good sir, this ring was given me by my wife,
　　And when she put it on, she made me vow
　　That I should neither sell, nor give, nor lose it.

PORTIA: That 'scuse serves many men to save their gifts.　440

443   *hold out enemy,* keep up her unfriendliness.

445   Do Portia and Nerissa depart in outraged dignity, aloof
       haughtiness, curt hostility, or struggling against laughter?

447   *valued 'gainst,* of sufficient value to sway you against.
       commandement. Four syllables.
          It is impossible for Bassanio to resist the request of the friend
       who so nearly died for him.

Venice

This scene elaborating the joke of the rings is a light tailpiece to the
previous one which on the Elizabethan stage it would have followed
without a break.

1   *deed,* i.e. deed of gift.

6   *advice,* consideration.

An if your wife be not a mad-woman,
And know how well I have deserved the ring,
She would not hold out enemy for ever
For giving it to me. Well, peace be with you.

[Exeunt Portia and Nerissa

ANTONIO: My Lord Bassanio, let him have the ring.
Let his deservings and my love withal
Be valued 'gainst your wife's commandement.
BASSANIO: Go Gratiano, run and overtake him,
Give him the ring, and bring him if thou canst
Unto Antonio's house; away, make haste.   *[Exit Gratiano*
Come, you and I will thither presently,   451
And in the morning early will we both
Fly toward Belmont. Come Antonio.   *[Exeunt*

SCENE TWO

Enter PORTIA and NERISSA

PORTIA: Inquire the Jew's house out, give him this deed,
And let him sign it; we'll away tonight,
And be a day before our husbands home.
This deed will be well welcome to Lorenzo.

Enter GRATIANO

GRATIANO: Fair sir, you are well o'erta'en.
My Lord Bassanio upon more advice,
Hath sent you here this ring, and doth entreat
Your company at dinner.
PORTIA: That cannot be.
His ring I do accept most thankfully,
And so I pray you tell him. Furthermore,   10

12   *That . . . do.* Gratiano moves as if to go while Nerissa speaks to Portia.

15   *old*, plenty of.

17   *outface them*, give them the lie. Possibly a hint that Bassanio and Antonio will not be able to recognize their faces.

I pray you show my youth old Shylock's house.

GRATIANO: That will I do.

NERISSA: Sir, I would speak with you.
   [*Aside to Portia*] I'll see if I can get my husband's ring
   Which I did make him swear to keep for ever.

PORTIA: [*Aside to Nerissa*] Thou mayst, I warrant. We shall have old swearing
   That they did give the rings away to men;
   But we'll outface them, and outswear them too.
   Away, make haste, thou know'st where I will tarry.

NERISSA: Come good sir, will you show me to this house?

                                                   [*Exeunt*

This scene opens with an incantation to charm away the tensions and agonies of the trial scene—'beauty making beautiful old rhyme in praise of ladies dead'. The famous lovers of ancient time are summoned, as it were, to approve a night for love and beauty and peace. The first twenty-two lines are musically arranged in antiphon, or if it is preferred, as variations on a theme. Should they be intoned or chanted?

The exchanges are also a game in which each tries to tease and outdo the other. Troilus refers to a faithless Cressida and Jessica retorts with Thisbe who was faithful to death and so on.

Some stage property is required (ll. 54–5).

4, 6   *Troilus, Cressid.* Troilus, a son of Priam, King of Troy, loved Cressida who returned his love. She was sent as a hostage to the camp of the besieging Greeks, where, in spite of her promise to be true to Troilus, she gave her love to a Greek, Deiphobus. These lines are based on Chaucer's poem *Troilus and Crisseyde*, ll. 647–75. The whole passage may have been inspired by Chaucer's *Legend of Good Women* which includes the stories of Thisbe, Dido and Medea.

7   *Thisbe.* The story of *Pyramus and Thisbe,* taken from Ovid's *Metamorphoses,* was the subject of the mechanicals' play in *A Midsummer Night's Dream.* The lovers who were forbidden to see each other by their parents, arranged to meet in a forest. Thisbe, frightened by a lion, ran away leaving behind her mantle which was mauled by the lion. Pyramus, assuming that Thisbe had been killed, stabbed himself. Thisbe, returning to find him dead, stabs herself with his sword.

9   *ran . . . away.* Sir J. T. Sheppard suggests that Jessica runs from Lorenzo at this point and standing on the bank (ll. 54–5) invites pursuit. He stands still reminding her of Dido teasingly implying that he is not pursuing her.

10   *Dido.* In Vergil's *Aeneid* the Queen of Carthage who loved Aeneas. He left her at the command of Jupiter and sailed on to found in Italy the family from which Julius Caesar and Augustus were descended.

     willow. The emblem of forsaken lovers.

11   *wild,* boundless, waste.

     waft, waved.

13   *Medea.* The daughter of the king of Colchis, who helped Jason with her spells to win the golden fleece. She eloped with him, and

ACT FIVE

SCENE ONE

Enter LORENZO *and* JESSICA

LORENZO: The moon shines bright. In such a night as this,
    When the sweet wind did gently kiss the trees,
    And they did make no noise, in such a night
    Troilus methinks mounted the Trojan walls,
    And sighed his soul toward the Grecian tents
    Where Cressid lay that night.
JESSICA: In such a night
    Did Thisbe fearfully o'ertrip the dew,
    And saw the lion's shadow ere himself,
    And ran dismayed away.
LORENZO: In such a night
    Stood Dido with a willow in her hand   10
    Upon the wild sea banks, and waft her love
    To come again to Carthage.
JESSICA: In such a night
    Medea gathered the enchanted herbs
    That did renew old Æson.

made Æson, Jason's father, young again by a brew of herbs gathered at the full moon. Jason proved a faithless husband and Medea poisoned his children and fled in a dragon-drawn chariot. Shakespeare probably remembered the details of the story in Golding's translation of Ovid's *Metamorphoses*. Jessica is perhaps implying that Lorenzo is sluggish in his love-making. He retorts by applying to her the other part of Medea's story, the elopement with Jason and the golden fleece.

15   *steal,* (*a*) depart secretly, (*b*) take dishonestly.

16   *unthrift,* unthrifty.

19   *Stealing,* winning, enticing. A glance back at 'steal' (l. 15). Jessica emphasizing the phrase, 'Stealing her soul' to imply that Lorenzo's is the worse crime. Possibly also a glance at her conversion to Christianity. Her tones possibly express a pout or mock grievance.

20–2   *In . . . her.* Any stage business?

21   *shrew,* i.e. a scandal-given little minx.

23   *out-night,* surpass you in illustrations of 'In such a night'.

24   *footing,* footsteps.

25   *so fast.* Stephano was running.

30–3   *she . . . maid.* Portia returns to her bridal night with humility and reverence.

31   *crosses.* Wayside crosses were then common.

39   *Sola.* Launcelot vociferously imitates the sound of a post-horn. He comes perhaps from within the house and has difficulty in finding Lorenzo.

Act Five, Scene One

LORENZO: In such a night
Did Jessica steal from the wealthy Jew,
And with an unthrift love did run from Venice,
As far as Belmont.

JESSICA: In such a night
Did young Lorenzo swear he loved her well,
Stealing her soul with many vows of faith,
And ne'er a true one.

LORENZO: In such a night   20
Did pretty Jessica, like a little shrew,
Slander her love, and he forgave it her.

JESSICA: I would out-night you did no body come.
But hark, I hear the footing of a man.

Enter STEPHANO

LORENZO: Who comes so fast in silence of the night?
STEPHANO: A friend.
LORENZO: A friend? What friend? Your name I pray you, friend?
STEPHANO: Stephano is my name, and I bring word
My mistress will before the break of day
Be here at Belmont; she doth stray about   30
By holy crosses where she kneels and prays
For happy wedlock hours.

LORENZO: Who comes with her?
STEPHANO: None but a holy hermit and her maid.
I pray you is my master yet returned?
LORENZO: He is not, nor we have not heard from him.
But go we in I pray thee Jessica,
And ceremoniously let us prepare
Some welcome for the mistress of the house.

Enter LAUNCELOT

LAUNCELOT: Sola, sola! Wo ha ho! Sola, sola!
LORENZO: Who calls?   40

46   *post,* courier, messenger.

47   *horn,* (*a*) post-horn, (*b*) cornucopia, horn of plenty. The 'post' wore a horn around his neck.

49   *expect,* await.

53   An unusual request. Presumably the musicians come down from the balcony and take up position at the back of the stage.

      Care in emphasizing the important lines in Lorenzo's two speeches with variations in speed is well repaid.

57   *Become,* are in keeping with.

      touches, playing, strains.

59   *patens,* (*a*) small circular dishes on which the bread is placed during the celebration of Holy Communion, (*b*) metal plates.

60–1 *There's . . . sings.* The Ptolemaic view of the universe placed the earth at the centre of transparent concentric spheres. In each sphere was 'inlaid' a certain planet or stars, and the movement of the outermost sphere caused day and night. The movement of these spheres produced notes which combined in perfect harmony which, however, could not be heard by mortals.

62   *still quiring,* ever singing together.

      young-eyed cherubins. The cherubim were above all other heavenly beings endowed with keenness of sight, *Ezekiel,* x. 12. Here young-eyed = with sight ever young.

63–5 *Such . . . it.* Immortal souls can appreciate this harmony (of the spheres) but while our immortal soul is enclosed in dull earthly, decaying bodies we cannot hear it. For 'harmony' = power to appreciate harmony see 'music' (l. 83) (Arden).

66   Possibly the musicians provided a consort of viols and played an 'ayre' softly until l. 109. Long suggests that, as the original music is not known, an 'ayre' by Campion, the 'Peaceful Western

Act Five, Scene One

LAUNCELOT: Sola! Did you see Master Lorenzo?
  Master Lorenzo, sola, sola!

LORENZO: Leave hollaing man, here.

LAUNCELOT: Sola! Where, where?

LORENZO: Here.

LAUNCELOT: Tell him there's a post come from my master,
  with his horn full of good news: my master will be here ere
  morning   [*Exit*

LORENZO: Sweet soul, let's in, and there expect their coming.
  And yet no matter—why should we go in?   50
  My friend Stephano, signify I pray you
  Within the house, your mistress is at hand,
  And bring your music forth into the air.   [*Exit Stephano*
  How sweet the moonlight sleeps upon this bank.
  Here will we sit, and let the sounds of music
  Creep in our ears. Soft stillness and the night
  Become the touches of sweet harmony.
  Sit Jessica. Look how the floor of heaven
  Is thick inlaid with patens of bright gold.
  There's not the smallest orb which thou behold'st   60
  But in his motion like an angel sings,
  Still quiring to the young-eyed cherubins;
  Such harmony is in immortal souls,
  But whilst this muddy vesture of decay
  Doth grossly close it in, we cannot hear it.

Enter Musicians

  Come ho, and wake Diana with a hymn,
  With sweetest touches pierce your mistress' ear,
  And draw her home with music.   [*Music*

Wind' may be appropriate (*Shakespeare's Use of Music*, p. 117). Lorenzo has described the celestial nature of harmony, now he speaks with musical accompaniment, an anticipation of recitative.

66   *wake*, i.e. keep the vigil of (Dover Wilson).
        Diana, the moon goddess.

70   *spirits*, mind.

72   *race*, drove, herd.

77   *mutual*, all together.

79   *poet*. Ovid, who tells the story in his *Metamorphoses*, X, XI.

80   *Orpheus*. In classical myth the famous musician whose music charmed not only living creatures but caused trees and rocks on Mount Olympus to follow him.

81   *stockish*, unfeeling.

83   *The . . . himself*, e.g. Shylock.

85   *spoils*, plundering.

86   *motions*, impulses.

87   *affections*, natural inclinations, nature.
        Erebus. A region of darkness near Hades, the dwelling place of the dead in classical myths.

90-1   *How...world*. Perhaps an echo of *St.Matthew*,v. 16,'Let your light so shine before men that they may see your good works', and 'Her candle goeth not out by night' of the virtuous woman of *Proverbs*, xxxi. 18.

       Portia's three proverbial remarks ll. 91, 93, 107-8, should be spoken deliberately.

91   *naughty*, wicked.

94   Again the deceptiveness of appearances (compare III. ii, 73 ff).

95   *state*, magnificence, dignity.

97   *main of waters*, ocean.

98   *music*, musicians.

99   *Nothing . . . respect*, nothing is absolutely good, its degree of goodness depends on the circumstances.

JESSICA: I am never merry when I hear sweet music.
LORENZO: The reason is your spirits are attentive.   70
    For do but note a wild and wanton herd,
    Or race of youthful and unhandled colts,
    Fetching mad bounds, bellowing and neighing loud,
    Which is the hot condition of their blood;
    If they but hear perchance a trumpet sound,
    Or any air of music touch their ears,
    You shall perceive them make a mutual stand,
    Their savage eyes turned to a modest gaze
    By the sweet power of music. Therefore the poet
    Did feign that Orpheus drew trees, stones, and floods;   80
    Since nought so stockish, hard, and full of rage,
    But music for the time doth change his nature.
    The man that hath no music in himself,
    Nor is not moved with concord of sweet sounds,
    Is fit for treasons, stratagems, and spoils;
    The motions of his spirit are dull as night,
    And his affections dark as Erebus:
    Let no such man be trusted. Mark the music.

Enter PORTIA *and* NERISSA

PORTIA: That light we see is burning in my hall.
    How far that little candle throws his beams,   90
    So shines a good deed in a naughty world.
NERISSA: When the moon shone we did not see the candle.
PORTIA: So doth the greater glory dim the less.
    A substitute shines brightly as a king
    Until a king be by, and then his state
    Empties itself, as doth an inland brook
    Into the main of waters. Music, hark.
NERISSA: It is your music madam of the house.
PORTIA: Nothing is good I see without respect,
    Methinks it sounds much sweeter than by day.   100

107   *by season*, by occurring at an appropriate time.
      seasoned, ripened, matured. A quibble on two meanings of 'season'

109   *Peace ho, the ... Endymion.* Portia calls on the musicians to cease,
      indicating again that the moon has set. Some editors prefer
      'Peace!—Low' following the 'Peace, Low' of the quarto and folio
      editions. Then, it is suggested, Portia silences Nerissa and points
      out Lorenzo and Jessica lying entranced on the moonlit bank—a
      very effective interpretation on the stage.
      Endymion. A beautiful youth with whom Selene, the moon, fell in
      love while he slept on Mount Latmos. She came down to kiss him
      and caused him to sleep perpetually on the mountain.

121   *tucket*, a flourish on a trumpet.

122   *trumpet.* Possibly each important person had his own trumpet call.

127–8 *We ... sun*, If you would walk in the night you would give such
      light that we should have day at the same time as people on the
      other side of the world. Bassanio follows up Portia's previous
      remark.

NERISSA: Silence bestows that virtue on it madam.

PORTIA: The crow doth sing as sweetly as the lark
  When neither is attended; and I think
  The nightingale, if she should sing by day
  When every goose is cackling, would be thought
  No better a musician than the wren.
  How many things by season seasoned are
  To their right praise and true perfection.
  Peace ho, the moon sleeps with Endymion,
  And would not be awaked.   *[Music ceases*

LORENZO: That is the voice,   110
  Or I am much deceived, of Portia.

PORTIA: He knows me as the blind man knows the cuckoo—
  By the bad voice.

LORENZO: Dear lady welcome home.

PORTIA: We have been praying for our husbands' welfare,
  Which speed, we hope, the better for our words.
  Are they returned?

LORENZO: Madam, they are not yet;
  But there is come a messenger before
  To signify their coming.

PORTIA: Go in Nerissa;
  Give order to my servants that they take
  No note at all of our being absent hence—   120
  Nor you, Lorenzo—Jessica, nor you.   *[A tucket sounds*

LORENZO: Your husband is at hand, I hear his trumpet.
  We are no tell-tales madam, fear you not.

PORTIA: This night methinks is but the daylight sick,
  It looks a little paler; 'tis a day,
  Such as the day is when the sun is hid.

Enter BASSANIO, ANTONIO, GRATIANO, *and their followers*

BASSANIO: We should hold day with the Antipodes,
  If you would walk in absence of the sun.

129   *light* (*a*) radiance, (*b*) wanton, (*c*) light (in weight).

130   *heavy*, sorrowful.

132   *sort*, dispose, arrange.

135   *infinitely bound*. An expressive and emphatic contradiction.

136   *in all sense*, (*a*) in all reason, (*b*) in every sense of the word.

136,   *bound.* (*a*) indebted, (*b*) in friendship.

137   (*a*) indebted, (*b*) pledged on oath (to Shylock), (*c*) imprisoned.

141   *scant . . . courtesy,* cease uttering mere words of welcome. Has some action preceded this?

146   *What's . . . matter?* Portia, of course, knows. How can she express this in feigning ignorance?

148   *posy*, motto engraved on the inner side of a ring.

150   *leave*, lose

156   *respective*, careful.

157   *Gave . . . clerk*. Does this sound a reasonable explanation?

158   *The . . . it*. Much of the fun of the rings' episode depends on dramatic irony, i.e. the words have frequently a double meaning perceived by Portia, Nerissa and the audience but not by Bassanio and Gratiano.

194

PORTIA: Let me give light, but let me not be light;
　　For a light wife doth make a heavy husband,　　　　　130
　　And never be Bassanio so for me.
　　But God sort all. You are welcome home my lord.
BASSANIO: I thank you madam. Give welcome to my friend.
　　This is the man, this is Antonio,
　　To whom I am so infinitely bound.
PORTIA: You should in all sense be much bound to him,
　　For as I hear he was much bound for you.
ANTONIO: No more than I am well acquitted of.
PORTIA: Sir, you are very welcome to our house.
　　It must appear in other ways than words,　　　　　140
　　Therefore I scant this breathing courtesy.
GRATIANO: [To Nerissa] By yonder moon I swear you do me
　　wrong,
　　In faith I gave it to the judge's clerk.
　　Would he were gelt that had it for my part,
　　Since you do take it so much at heart.
PORTIA: A quarrel ho, already? What's the matter?
GRATIANO: About a hoop of gold, a paltry ring
　　That she did give me, whose posy was
　　For all the world like cutler's poetry
　　Upon a knife, 'Love me, and leave me not'.　　　　　150
NERISSA: What talk you of the posy or the value?
　　You swore to me when I did give it you,
　　That you would wear it till your hour of death,
　　And that it should lie with you in your grave.
　　Though not for me, yet for your vehement oaths,
　　You should have been respective and have kept it.
　　Gave it a judge's clerk? No, God's my judge,
　　The clerk will ne'er wear hair on's face that had it.
GRATIANO: He will, an if he live to be a man.
NERISSA: Ay, if a woman live to be a man.　　　　　160
GRATIANO: Now by this hand I gave it to a youth,

162 *scrubbed*, dwarfish, stunted.

164 *prating*, talkative, chattering.
     How do Nerissa and Bassanio receive this description?

171 *and . . . stands.* How is Bassanio standing? Any movement or
     posture? How does Gratiano take this?

174 *masters*, possesses.

176 *And*, if.

179– *My . . . too*, Gratiano enjoys Bassanio's discomfort and perhaps a
81   little maliciously gives him away.

A kind of boy, a little scrubbed boy,
No higher than thyself, the judge's clerk,
A prating boy that begged it as a fee.
I could not for my heart deny it him.

PORTIA: You were to blame, I must be plain with you,
To part so slightly with your wife's first gift,
A thing stuck on with oaths upon your finger,
And riveted with faith unto your flesh.
I gave my love a ring, and made him swear   170
Never to part with it, and here he stands.
I dare be sworn for him he would not leave it,
Nor pluck it from his finger, for the wealth
That the world masters. Now in faith Gratiano,
You give your wife too unkind a cause of grief.
And't were to me I should be mad at it.

BASSANIO: [*Aside*] Why I were best to cut my left hand off,
And swear I lost the ring defending it.

GRATIANO: My Lord Bassanio gave his ring away
Unto the judge that begged it, and indeed   180
Deserved it too. And then the boy his clerk
That took some pains in writing, he begged mine,
And neither man nor master would take aught
But the two rings.

PORTIA: What ring gave you, my lord?
Not that I hope which you received of me.

BASSANIO: If I could add a lie unto a fault,
I would deny it; but you see my finger
Hath not the ring upon it, it is gone.

PORTIA: Even so void is your false heart of truth.
By heaven I will ne'er come in your bed   190
Until I see the ring.

NERISSA: Nor I in yours
Till I again see mine.

BASSANIO: Sweet Portia,

197

193ff. *If . . . ring.* What feeling prompts this repetition: lightheartedness, teasing, emphasis, serious pleading, anxiety, mock-dismay, attempt-to-jolly-his-way-out-of-it?

199 *virtue,* power. Portia answers Bassanio with mocking imitation of his plea.

201 *contain,* retain.

205–6 *wanted . . . ceremony,* so lacking in moderation that he would have pressed for a thing held as a sacred symbol.

210 *civil doctor,* (*a*) a doctor of civil law, (*b*) a courteous, gentlemanly doctor.

216 *I . . . enforced.* Bassanio does not mention Antonio's part in the matter.

226 *liberal,* (*a*) generous, (*b*) unfaithful.

If you did know to whom I gave the ring,
If you did know for whom I gave the ring,
And would conceive for what I gave the ring
And how unwillingly I left the ring,
When nought would be accepted but the ring,
You would abate the strength of your displeasure.

PORTIA: If you had known the virtue of the ring,
  Or half her worthiness that gave the ring,   200
  Or your own honour to contain the ring,
  You would not then have parted with the ring.
  What man is there so much unreasonable,
  If you had pleased to have defended it
  With any terms of zeal, wanted the modesty
  To urge the thing held as a ceremony?
  Nerissa teaches me what to believe:
  I'll die for't, but some woman had the ring.

BASSANIO: No by my honour madam, by my soul
  No woman had it, but a civil doctor,   210
  Which did refuse three thousand ducats of me,
  And begged the ring, the which I did deny him,
  And suffered him to go displeased away,
  Even he that did uphold the very life
  Of my dear friend. What should I say sweet lady?
  I was enforced to send it after him.
  I was beset with shame and courtesy;
  My honour would not let ingratitude
  So much besmear it. Pardon me good lady,
  For by these blessed candles of the night,   220
  Had you been there, I think you would have begged
  The ring of me to give the worthy doctor.

PORTIA: Let not that doctor e'er come near my house.
  Since he hath got the jewel that I loved,
  And that which you did swear to keep for me,
  I will become as liberal as you;

230   *Argus.* In classical story a person with a hundred eyes, renowned for his watchfulness.

240   *enforced,* i.e. which I was obliged to do.

244–6 *In . . . credit.* Portia suggests that Bassanio would be guilty of double-dealing. Her teasing now becomes obvious.

246   *oath of credit.* Ironical.

249   *wealth,* prosperity.

249–   Antonio again offers himself, this time his soul in pledge for
54   Bassanio's faith.

251   *miscarried,* been lost.

253   *advisedly,* deliberately. Bassanio had given the ring 'upon more advice'.

I'll not deny him anything I have,
No, not my body, nor my husband's bed.
Know him I shall, I am well sure of it.
Lie not a night from home. Watch me like Argus.   230
If you do not, if I be left alone,
Now by mine honour, which is yet mine own,
I'll have that doctor for my bedfellow.

NERISSA: And I his clerk. Therefore be well advised
How you do leave me to mine own protection.

GRATIANO: Well do you so. Let me not take him then,
For if I do, I'll mar the young clerk's pen.

ANTONIO: I am the unhappy subject of these quarrels.

PORTIA: Sir, grieve not you, you are welcome notwithstanding.

BASSANIO: Portia, forgive me this enforced wrong,   240
And in the hearing of these many friends
I swear to thee, even by thine own fair eyes
Wherein I see myself—

PORTIA: Mark you but that?
In both my eyes he doubly sees himself,
In each eye, one—swear by your double self,
And there's an oath of credit.

BASSANIO: Nay, but hear me.
Pardon this fault, and by my soul I swear
I never more will break an oath with thee.

ANTONIO: I once did lend my body for his wealth,
Which but for him that had your husband's ring   250
Had quite miscarried. I dare be bound again,
My soul upon the forfeit, that your lord
Will never more break faith advisedly.

PORTIA: Then you shall be his surety. Give him this,
And bid him keep it better than the other.

ANTONIO: Here Lord Bassanio, swear to keep this ring.

BASSANIO: By heaven it is the same I gave the doctor.

PORTIA: I had it of him. Pardon me Bassanio,

259   *lay*, lodged.

261   *same . . . boy*. A hit at Gratiano's account. Spoken with delibera-
tion and emphasis.

263–4 *Why . . . enough*. This is like the mending of ways under circumstances in which there is no need of mending.

     All this to-do is unnecessary, you accused us of being untrue
with the idea of mending our ways and your own ways are no
better.

263   *mending of highways*, with perhaps a glance at 'mending one's
ways'.

265   *cuckolds*, husbands whose wives have been untrue.

266   *grossly*, coarsely. Portia puts Gratiano firmly into place.

278–9 *You shall . . . letter*. See Introduction, p.13.

286   *living*, livelihood, means of living.

288   *road*, anchorage.

For by this ring the doctor lay with me.

NERISSA: And pardon me my gentle Gratiano, 260
For that same scrubbed boy the doctor's clerk,
In lieu of this last night did lie with me.

GRATIANO: Why this is like the mending of highways
In summer where the ways are fair enough.
What, are we cuckolds ere we have deserved it?

PORTIA: Speak not so grossly. You are all amazed.
Here is a letter, read it at your leisure—
It comes from Padua from Bellario—
There you shall find that Portia was the doctor,
Nerissa there her clerk. Lorenzo here 270
Shall witness I set forth as soon as you,
And even but now returned. I have not yet
Entered my house. Antonio you are welcome,
And I have better news in store for you
Than you expect. Unseal this letter soon,
There you shall find three of your argosies
Are richly come to harbour suddenly.
You shall not know by what strange accident
I chanced on this letter.

ANTONIO: I am dumb.

BASSANIO: Were you the doctor, and I knew you not? 280

GRATIANO: Were you the clerk that is to make me cuckold?

NERISSA: Ay but the clerk that never means to do it,
Unless he live until he be a man.

BASSANIO: Sweet doctor, you shall be my bedfellow.
When I am absent, then lie with my wife.

ANTONIO: Sweet lady, you have given me life and living;
For here I read for certain that my ships
Are safely come to road.

PORTIA: How now Lorenzo?
My clerk hath some good comforts too for you.

NERISSA: Ay, and I'll give them him without a fee. 290

298 *charge . . . inter'gatories,* and there make us swear on oath to answer your questions. A flash of humour in a last legal phrase at her legal exploits.

    There do I give to you and Jessica
    From the rich Jew, a special deed of gift
    After his death, of all he dies possessed of.
LORENZO: Fair ladies, you drop manna in the way
    Of starved people.
PORTIA: It is almost morning,
    And yet I am sure you are not satisfied
    Of these events at full. Let us go in,
    And charge us there upon inter'gatories,
    And we will answer all things faithfully.
GRATIANO: Let it be so. The first inter'gatory   300
    That my Nerissa shall be sworn on is,
    Whether till the next night she had rather stay,
    Or go to bed now, being two hours to day.
    But were the day come, I should wish it dark
    That I were couching with the doctor's clerk.
    Well, while I live I'll fear no other thing
    So sore, as keeping safe Nerissa's ring.   *[Exeunt*

APPENDICES

I

THE SOURCES OF *THE MERCHANT OF VENICE*

SHAKESPEARE as usual is well acquainted with several versions of the story he used as his source for the main plot. Either he read all the versions he could lay hands on in preparation for writing the play, or he read widely and remembered what he read.

He owes most to an Italian tale in Ser Giovanni's *Il Pecorone*, published in Milan in 1558, though the collection of stories was written in the 14th century. Some scholars maintain that Shakespeare read the story in the original Italian for no English or French version was available; others suggest that there was an English version now lost, and that a play, *The Jew*, which was acted before 1579 may have been an early dramatic version upon which Shakespeare drew. Whichever way it was, there are numerous phrases in *The Merchant of Venice* which are translated direct from the original. The following is a summary of the story from *Il Pecorone*.

Giannetto was the beloved godson of Ansaldo, the richest Christian merchant in Venice. During a voyage he learnt of the beautiful, wealthy lady of the port of Belmont, and how all strangers were expected to attempt to win her; failure, however, meant the loss of the suitor's possessions. Giannetto undertook to win her, but she gave him drugged wine and he failed. To explain his losses Giannetto told Ansaldo that he had been shipwrecked, and Ansaldo equipped him for a second voyage. Again Giannetto was drugged and lost everything. Ansaldo obtained the money to equip Giannetto a third time by borrowing from a Jew on condition that the Jew might cut off a pound of flesh from his body if he failed to pay by St. John's day. This time, Giannetto, warned by a maid that the wine was drugged, poured it down his breast and won the lady. He married her and ruled over Belmont in great happiness.

The festivities of St. John's day reminded him of Ansaldo's pledge. Alarmed and anxious he set out for Venice furnished with money by his lady. In the meantime the Jew has seized Ansaldo and refused the offers of other merchants to pay the debt, demanding as his legal right the pound of flesh.

The lady of Belmont, dressed as a doctor of law, followed Giannetto to Venice. Giannetto took the Jew to the doctor, not knowing who the doctor was, to obtain legal opinion on the bond. As the Jew remained inflexible, the case was referred to a court. To Giannetto's dismay the doctor told the Jew to take the pound of flesh to which he was entitled. Then she added, as the Jew approached Ansaldo with a razor in his hand, that if he took a drop of Ansaldo's blood, his head would be cut off. Repeated requests by the Jew for some portion of his money were refused, only the pound of flesh was to be taken at his peril. The Jew tore the bond in pieces and was mocked out of court. Giannetto offered the doctor the money he had brought, but the lawyer refused it. However, seeing a ring on Giannetto's finger, he asked for it. Giannetto gave it, saying that he did so unwillingly because it had been given him by his wife whom he loved dearly.

The lady returned to Belmont a few days before Giannetto explaining that she had been to the baths. When he arrived she treated him coldly, accusing him of giving away her ring to a former lady-love in Venice. Giannetto swore that he had given the ring to the lawyer; the lady retorted that he had given it to a woman. Thereupon Giannetto burst into tears. Relenting, the lady embraced him and laughingly showed him the ring and explained that she was the lawyer. They were joyously reunited. Giannetto gave the maid who warned him of the drugged wine to Ansaldo for his wife.

It will be noticed that this story does not contain the casket method of winning the lady, nor an appeal for mercy, nor any reference to an elopement, nor the forced conversion of the Jew to Christianity.

Other stories probably provided some of this material. Anthony Munday's *Zelauto*, 1580, contains a bond story and a trial which is not in general so close to *The Merchant of Venice*, as the story of Giannetto, but it does contain an appeal to the Gentile usurer to have mercy as he is a Christian and hopes for salvation. There are also a few phrases that reappear in *The Merchant of Venice*. Similarly, a ballad *Gernutus* of uncertain date has the expression 'merry jest' for the bond and describes the Jew whetting his knife. The *Orator*, 1596, a translation from the French of

The Sources of The Merchant of Venice

Alexander Silvayn, gives the argument of a Jew 'who would for his debt have a pound of flesh of a Christian' and the Christian's reply. Shylock's arguments in court about slavery and his preference for the pound of flesh rather than money may come from this source. A casket story occurs in the *Gesta Romanorum*, a famous collection of Latin stories frequently translated. The inscriptions on the gold and silver caskets are similar to those in the play but are interchanged, and the caskets contain in order, a dead man's bones, earth and worms, and jewels. The daughter of the King of Ampluy makes the correct choice by which she proves her worthiness to marry the son of the Emperor of Rome. The story is an allegory and a moral is appended.

Marlowe's tragedy, *The Jew of Malta*, c. 1589, certainly influenced Shakespeare. There are similarities in phrasing, and the villainous Barabas and his daughter Abigail who turns Christian no doubt suggested Shylock and Jessica.

Apart from the allegory in the *Gesta Romanorum* and the savage malice of Barabas in *The Jew of Malta*, the sources have a light entertainment value as of stories told to an audience where clever intrigue, wit and immediacy are important. There is no probing of motive or emotion, no challenging moral issues. Yet it is precisely these things lacking in the sources that are so prominent in *The Merchant of Venice*. All this Shakespeare may have created for himself, but it is certain that he knew of a medieval story (*All's Well*, III. iv, 25-9) in which the Virgin Mary or Mercy pleaded for mercy for mankind before the throne of God, and which might have prompted a deeper tone.

This medieval story usually referred to as the *Four Daughters of God*, or in another form as the *Processus Belial* (*Sathanae* or *Luciferae*) was extremely popular throughout Christendom. It exists in prose story, in verse (*Piers Plowman*), in painting, in sermon, and in several morality plays particularly in France and England. Indeed, its theme of Judgement is one of the major themes of the morality plays.

The Four Daughters of God, Mercy, Truth, Justice (Righteousness) and Peace to whom a fifth Sapience (Wisdom) has been added appear before God in the court of Heaven. Mankind is summoned at the insistence of Justice who demands that he shall pay the penalty for his sins. After some delay Sapience is asked to decide the issue. At first she appears to side with Justice, but Mercy pleads that Mankind should be spared if he makes a penance or if a substitute dies for him. Sapience then pleads for mercy on the ground that without God's mercy no one would obtain salvation. Justice accepts the plea and there is general rejoicing and angelic singing in Heaven.

In the other version the Devil appears before God in the court of Heaven and demands that because of his sinfulness Mankind shall be given to him. For a time his claim seems likely to succeed because there is no one to speak for the accused. Finally the Virgin Mary consents to defend him. The Devil stresses the justice of his demand, and that God, who is justice, must therefore side with him. Mary pleads for mercy arguing that mercy is also of God and that therefore justice must be tempered with mercy. The Devil then produces scales and demands that the portion of Mankind that is due to him should be weighed and given to him if he cannot have all. This is denied him and he is driven out of Heaven in humiliation.

One painting on this subject is the Judgement of Adam and Eve, 1681, by Johan Lauw in the National Museum, Helsinki, part of which is reproduced on page 211.

In the heavenly court of law God stands holding orb and sceptre behind the table, on his righthand is Jesus, above them is the Holy Ghost as a dove. On God's lefthand under the sword of justice stands Justice with scales and Truth with a try-square, both counsel for the plaintiff, Satan. On Christ's righthand under an olive branch stands Mercy clasping her hands and Peace bearing another olive branch. In front before the bar Adam and Eve are entwined by the serpent whose tail is held by Satan. Satan with furry legs and tail, talons for hands and an ape-like face is gesticulating and calling on God to pass judgement on Adam and Eve. Truth and Justice argue that Adam and Eve were warned not to eat of the tree and must as sinners receive punishment. Mercy asks for God's mercy, and Peace asks Christ to show pity by deeds. Christ acknowledges that he must die for mankind. On the table are the decalogue, the apple, and a scroll declaring that repentance pleases God more than the death of a sinner.

S. C. Chew, from whose book, *The Virtues Reconciled*, pp. 66–8, the above is summarized with a slight addition, writes: 'The presence of Diabolus to argue his case and press his claim, connects this painting with the dramatic form of the allegory called the *Processus Belial*'; and again:

'It is likely that this painting is a reasonably exact representation of the Parliament of Heaven as it was enacted in the German mystery plays, and so takes us fairly close to . . . the English Salutation and Conception play of the Coventry cycle, and to *The Castle of Perseverance*.'

THE JUDGEMENT OF ADAM AND EVE
from the painting by Johan Lauw, 1681
(*By courtesy of the National Museum, Finland*)

II

THE JEWS IN SHAKESPEARE'S DAY

JEWS were officially expelled from England in 1290, yet in Shakespeare's time there were Jews living in London, probably many of them being Spanish in origin. As long as they outwardly conformed to Christianity no particular hostility was shown towards them. In 1594 there was an outburst of anti-Jewish feeling during and after the trial and execution of Roderigo Lopez, Queen Elizabeth's physician. Lopez, however, had been living a highly respected and trusted man until the enmity of the Earl of Essex ruined him. Most of the Jews lived either in Italy or in Turkey. In Italy they lived in ghettoes despised, ill-treated and in fear of the Inquisition; in Turkey they flourished as free citizens.

The Jew who appeared in Elizabethan writings is not a contemporary figure, he is a stock figure derived from the legends and plays of the Middle Ages in which he appears as an extortioner, an agent of the devil and given to ritual murder of children. Thus although Marlowe's play *The Jew of Malta* owes something to a real historical figure, Joseph, Duke of Naxos, Marlowe, naming him Barabas, has completely falsified his character and drawn him according to the medieval pattern as a monster of evil. Whether Shakespeare was influenced in creating Shylock by Lopez as some maintain, or whether he knew other Jews in London, is not known. The basis for Shylock was the traditional one, the humanity of the character is Shakespeare's addition.

III

SHAKESPEARE'S THEATRE

THE first public theatres in London were built during Shakespeare's life-time, but they embodied in their design and construction the experience and practice of the medieval and Tudor play productions in inn yards and elsewhere.

From square, circular or hexagonal theatre walls tiered with galleries for spectators, the Elizabethan stage jutted out over six feet above ground level and occupied about half the floor space where the spectators could stand on three sides of it. The stage of the Fortune theatre was 43 feet × 27 feet and the floor area in which it stood was 55 feet × 55 feet. At the back of the stage the lowest tier of spectators' galleries gave place to a curtained recess or inner stage used for interior scenes. On either side were dressing rooms from which entrance doors opened on to the stage. The first floor gallery behind the stage was used as a balcony for musicians or for scenes in the play, if it was not required for these purposes, spectators used it. Above the balcony and covering the rear portion of the stage was a canopy or roof painted blue and adorned with stars supported by pillars from the stage. There were trap doors in the stage and frequently a low rail around it.

The pillars, canopy, railings and back stage were painted and adorned. If a tragedy was to be performed, the stage was hung with black, but there was no set staging in the modern fashion.

There were stage properties usually of the kind that could be easily pushed on and off the stage. Records of the time mention a mossy bank, a wall, a bed, trees, arbours, thrones, tents, rock, tomb, hell-mouth, a cauldron; on the other hand pavilions and mansions may have been permanent 'sets' in some historical plays. On the whole properties were limited to essentials although the popularity of the private masques with their painted canvas sets encouraged increasing elaboration of scenery and spectacle during the reign of James I.

There was no limitation to the display of rich and gorgeous costumes

THE GLOBE THEATRE
A reconstruction by Dr J. C. Adams and Irwin Smith

in the current fashion of the day. The more magnificent and splendid the better; indeed the costumes must have been the most expensive item in the requirements of the company. An occasional attempt was made at period costume, but normally plays were produced in Elizabethan garments without any suspicion of the oddness that strikes us when we read of Caesar entering 'in his nightshirt' or Cleopatra calling on Charmian to cut the lace of what we may call her corsets. High rank was marked by magnificence of dress, a trade or calling by functional clothes. Feste, the clown, would wear the traditional fool's coat or petticoat of motley, a coarse cloth of mixed yellow and green. The coat was buttoned from the neck to the girdle from which hung a wooden dagger. Its skirts voluminous with capacious pockets in which Feste might 'impetticoat' any gratillity'. Ghosts, who appear in a number of plays wore a kind of leathern smock. Oberon and magicians such as Prospero wore, in the delightful phrase and spelling of the records, 'a robe for to goo invisibell'.

The actors formed companies under the patronage of noblemen for protection against a civic law condemning them as 'rogues, vagabonds and sturdy beggars' to severe punishment. They were the servants of their patron and wore his livery. The company was a co-operative society, its members jointly owned the property and shared the profits; thus Shakespeare's plays were not his to use as he liked, they belonged to his company, the Lord Chamberlain's Men. This company, honoured by James I when it became the King's Men, was the most successful company of the period. It had a number of distinguished actors, it achieved more Court performances than any other company, and it performed in the best London theatre, the Globe, until it was burnt down during a performance of *Henry VIII* in 1613. Women were not allowed on the public stage, although they performed in masques and theatricals in private houses. Boys, therefore, were apprenticed to the leading actors and took the female parts.

The audience in the public theatres was drawn from all classes. There were courtiers and inns of court men who appreciated intricate word play, mythological allusions and the technique of sword play; there were the 'groundlings' who liked jigs, horse-play and flamboyance of speech and spectacle; and there were the citizens who appreciated the romantic stories, the high eloquence of patriotic plays and moral sentiments. A successful play would have something for all. Sometimes gallants would sit on a stool on the stage and behave rather like the courtiers in *A Midsummer Night's Dream*, V.i, or *Love's Labour's Lost*, V.ii. The 'groundlings' too were likely to be troublesome and noisy. They could buy bottled-beer, oranges and nuts for their comfort; but it is noted to their credit that when Falstaff appeared on the stage, so popular was he that they stopped cracking nuts! They applauded a well delivered speech; they hissed a boring play; they even rioted and severely damaged one theatre. Shakespeare's plays however were popular among all classes: at Court they

did so take Eliza and our James,

and elsewhere in the public theatre they outshone the plays of other dramatists. Any play of his was assured of a 'full house'. An ardent theatre-goer of the day praising Shakespeare's plays above those of other dramatists wrote:

> When let but Falstaff come,
> Hal, Poins, the rest, you scarce shall have a room,
> All is so pester'd; let but Beatrice
> And Benedick be seen, lo in a trice
> The cockpit, galleries, boxes, all are full
> To hear Malvolio, that cross-garter'd gull.

Shakespeare's Works

The year of composition of only a few of Shakespeare's plays can be determined with certainty. The following list is based on current scholarly opinion.

The plays marked with an asterisk were not included in the First Folio edition of Shakespeare's plays (1623) which was prepared by Heminge and Condell, Shakespeare's fellow actors. Shakespeare's part in them has been much debated.

1590–1   2 Henry VI, 3 Henry VI.
1591–2   1 Henry VI.
1592–3   Richard III, Comedy of Errors.
1593–4   Titus Andronicus, Taming of the Shrew, Sir Thomas More* (Part authorship. Four manuscript pages presumed to be in Shakespeare's hand).
1594–5   Two Gentlemen of Verona, Love's Labour's Lost, Romeo and Juliet, Edward III* (Part authorship).
1595–6   Richard II, A Midsummer Night's Dream.
1596–7   King John, Merchant of Venice, Love's Labour Won (Not extant. Before 1598).
1597–8   1 Henry IV, 2 Henry IV, The Merry Wives of Windsor.
1598–9   Much Ado About Nothing, Henry V.
1599–1600   Julius Caesar, As You Like It.
1600–1   Hamlet, Twelfth Night.
1601–2   Troilus and Cressida.
1602–3   All's Well that Ends Well.